S0-BHX-942

TOWERING TEXAN

a Biography of

THOMAS J. RUSK

by

CLEBURNE HUSTON

44280

TEXIAN PRESS   ●   WACO, TEXAS   ●   1971

J. M. HODGES LEARNING CENTER
WHARTON COUNTY JUNIOR COLLEGE
WHARTON, TEXAS 77488

Copyright 1971
By Texian Press

Library of Congress Catalog Card Number
75-135345

Published by

Bound by
Library Binding Co.
Waco, Texas

923.2764
R.897t

44280

DEDICATED

to My Wife, Bess,

for Efficient Assistance and

Constant Encouragement

iii

Introduction

A towering figure, physically and mentally, Thomas Jefferson Rusk strode through the strife and turmoil of the convulsive years of the creation of Texas. Unswayed by personal ambition and aloof from petty jealousies and quarrels rampant on all sides, Rusk, for 22 years, had a firm hand in almost every development in the War for Independence, the formation and nurturing of the bold Republic and the difficult early years of statehood.

Through the productive years of his life, he devoted almost full time to the service of the land he loved, driven by a sense of loyalty and duty, rather than a yen for public acclaim. The people wanted him for President of Texas, but he modestly declined, feeling that his services were not required in that position.

Rusk was associated with all the great men of Texas in those perilous years and was admired by nearly all, though he did not hesitate to cross sharply, high or low, when principles of justice or the welfare of Texas were involved. He was a man without fear, whether in war or in the confrontations of political affairs.

In the United States Senate for eleven years, he matched wits with such giants as Daniel Webster, Henry Clay, John C. Calhoun, William H. Seward and other great men of the nation, and came off well in his fight for the welfare of his beloved Texas. Some of the members of the Congress, observing his talent as a peacemaker, thought of him for President of the United States, hoping that he might, by some miracle, close the chasm which in the 1850's was splitting the nation asunder, driving it to fratricidal war. But at the height of his fame and influence, disaster struck and he died a tragic death.

Being human, Rusk had his faults, but, as well said by his associate, Sam Houston: "If he had infirmities, they were few in proportion to those which fall to the lot of man." He was the most universally popular figure in Texas during his lifetime, but due to his modesty and disinterest in public acclaim, he has been overshadowed in written history by his more dramatic and controversial contemporary and friend, Sam Houston.

The author has made a conscientious effort to present Thomas J. Rusk in his true light and his proper place in history, unbiased by the writer's own admiration for this great Texas patriot.

THE AUTHOR

Stamford, Texas
1971

Acknowledgments

Among the rewarding experiences in the research on Thomas J. Rusk have been the contacts with a number of alert, refined and friendly people. At Stephen F. Austin State University, President R. W. Steen made Rusk pictures available. Miss Mildred Wyatt, director of Special Collections in the Library, was especially helpful in drawing out Rusk files and assisting in locating essential papers. Dr. Archie P. McDonald of the History Department offered helpful suggestions and Mrs. Lois Hale, curator of the Old Stone Fort, assisted with pictures and relics in the Rusk room.

Elsewhere in Nacogdoches, Mrs. Guy A. Blount, authority on Rusk history, was most gracious and helpful, and at the Court House, Mrs. Hope Skipper, County Clerk, and her staff searched out needed documents.

In Austin, Dr. John Kinney, archivist, of the State Library, and his staff cooperated in every way possible. The richest source of materials is the Rusk Papers in the University of Texas Archives. Dr. Chester V. Kielman, archivist, and his staff were helpful to the author in making most effective use of this valuable collection.

The McMurry College Library, Abilene, was a convenient source of background material and has a complete file of the *Texas State Historical Association* and *Southwestern Historical* Quarterlies. Dr. Joe Easterly is the efficient and courteous librarian. Research was also carried on in the Hardin-Simmons University Library, Abilene, which has the bulky files of the *Congressional Globe*. Useful reference works were found in the writer's home town, the Carnegie Library of Stamford, Mrs. Hollis Payne, librarian. Some hours were spent in the Louisiana State University Library at Baton Rouge, which has an extensive Texas history section.

Contents

Illustrations

(Following Page 84)

CHAPTER 1

The Foreigner Rusk on a Fool's Errand

Dejected and bone-weary, a bedraggled horseman traveled through the East Texas forest along the rough, muddy road euphoniously called el Camino Real. It was mid-January, 1835, and the slanting rays of the sun barely penetrated the heavy growth of stately virgin pines, interspaced with naked oaks, blackjacks and hickories. Occasionally the lone traveler might leave the rutted road to ride on the soft carpet of fallen leaves and pine needles along the wayside. He was oblivious to the primitive beauty of the surroundings, but noticed absently the reddish sand-and-clay soil of the Texas Redlands which reminded him of his Georgia homeland.

Between San Augustine and Nacogdoches, el Camino Real (the King's Highway) undulated over hills and valleys, across streams, past scattered farmsteads. It was along this route, also known as the Old San Antonio Road, that dauntless priests of centuries past had traveled to the missions at Nacogdoches and San Antonio de Bexar. Here the filibusters, Spanish soldiers and roving Indians had trod. This way the settlers from the southeastern states of the North American Republic had journeyed with families, livestock and household effects to San Felipe to take up land in Stephen F. Austin's well-regulated colony. Over this route had come fleeing criminals and crooked gamblers who were now labled G. T. T. (gone to Texas) in their former abode in the United States.

The dejected traveler was neither priest, prospector, gambler nor freebooter. He was the young lawyer, Thomas Jefferson Rusk, in pursuit of fugitives who had cheated him out of his last dollar. He, like many others, had invested his small fortune in a mining venture in the "gold rush" in Georgia. The promoters had "gone to Texas," carrying with them all the funds of the mining company.

Angry and despondent, Rusk had taken off in pursuit, leaving his young family behind. The entire route he followed is not known. Many travelers made the long trip overland from Georgia to Texas, crossing wide rivers and narrower streams by ferries and fords. Some took the water route, sailing to New Orleans, thence by steamboat up the Mississippi and the Red River to Natchitoches, Louisiana, the twin-sister of Nacogdoches, Texas, though miles apart.

Either way, Rusk would have arrived at Natchitoches, there to follow el Camino Real, crossing the international boundary, the Sabine River, at Gaines Ferry into Mexican territory, continuing the route through the new shack town of San Augustine, past the Halfway House and on to Nacogdoches. The overland trip from Georgia to Texas normally required four weeks or longer. Nacogdoches was the entry port for land travelers from the east. Those who came by sea could land at Galveston or Velasco and would find themselves in a much different kind of Texas.

Rusk's better judgment must have told him from the start that this was a wild-goose chase, but something from within had driven him on. It might have been partly a matter of injured pride that he, an able lawyer, had allowed himself to be swindled in a fraudulent mining venture. Besides he was being hounded at home for his debts and his folly, and this provided a temporary retreat. Possibly there was also a secret desire to see the "Promised Land" called Texas.

Now as he continued to ride westward, and having set foot on the foreign land that looked so much like Georgia, Thomas J. Rusk was doubtless conscious in his own mind that the long, weary trip was indeed a fool's errand. How could he hope to trap three paltry crooks in the great expanses of Texas where so many fugitives had escaped? And what might he recover if he did find them?

In spite of the shabbiness of most of the houses in town, Nacogdoches had some definite marks of civilization. The most imposing structure was the so-called Stone Fort, already old, having been built by Gil y'Barbo about 1779. There were a few comfortable homes owned by such solid citizens as Henry Raguet, Adolphus Sterne and others. The town was headquarters of the Mexican Government for the wide Redlands district of eastern Texas.

Rusk was relieved to see some signs of comfort in the town; he might stop a few days before going farther or returning

2

home. He left his mud-stained horse at the livery stable to be watered, fed, groomed and stalled. He probably made a few discreet inquiries as to who might have arrived recently from Georgia. Then he sought lodging which he may have found at Brown's Tavern on the plaza, patronized chiefly by Anglo-Americans, or at Cantina del Monte, owned by Senor Miguel Cortenoz. His best source of information likely would have been at the Monte, where dancing and gambling went on most of the night. Somewhere at least, Rusk got wind that his former associates were in town—and the culprits doubtless learned of their pursuer's arrival. At least one of the fugitives was overtaken at the outskirts of town, but it was an empty haul.

Clever enough to filch the fortune of a Georgia lawyer, the embezzlers were not smart enough to deal with Texas card sharks who had relieved many a newcomer of his cash. The Georgia crooks had lost all of Rusk's money in a card game. Nacogdoches, besides other claims to fame, was known as a "gamblers' heaven" and might have deserved the distinction. Rusk was able to detain at least one of the men for a time, but there is no record of his recovering any of the embezzled funds.[1]

Even in Nacogdoches, where strangers were coming and going all the time and it was bad manners to ask one's business, the arrival of Thomas J. Rusk could hardly go unnoticed. His striking personal appearance at this time is described by the historian, John Henry Brown, as "tall and commanding in presence, with dark complexion, deep-set and benevolent eyes, manly and kindly features, beaming with nobility of soul . . . A single glance at his splendid presence won every heart, and the whole people took him on trust."[2] A lock of hair which has been preserved in the Rusk Room of the Old Stone Fort is of a reddish brown and family papers show that he was sometimes called "Red".

Two such striking personalities as Sam Houston and Thomas J. Rusk could not have remained long in the same town without meeting. Whether Rusk sought out Houston for legal advice, or if the affable Houston made the first contact, is not clear. "Don Pablo Houston", as he then styled himself, had arrived in Texas two years before and, after traveling about a bit

---

[1]Texas Almanac of 1858 from A Compendium of Texas History, compiled by James M. Day (Texian Press, Waco, 1967) p. 60. This episode is related by a number of different sources with minor variations.
[2]Brown, John Henry, The Encyclopedia of the New West, pp. 739-40.

and sending a report to President Andrew Jackson, had taken up residence in Nacogdoches. There he was pursuing the role of a good citizen of Mexico, living down some of his past, practicing law and courting the attractive Miss Anna Raguet. At the time of Rusk's arrival, he was trying a land case in Judge Juan Mora's court.[3]

The meeting of the two Anglo-American lawyers quickly developed into a lasting friendship. The destiny which brought Thomas J. Rusk and Sam Houston together by chance in Nacogdoches, in the Mexican state of Coahuila y Texas, was to shape the history of a new republic spreading from the Sabine to the Rio Grande, and bring repercussions from Washington, D. C., to Mexico City and even to California and the Pacific shores. The two great men were destined to fight side by side at San Jacinto, to labor together in establishing the Republic of Texas, eventually to secure annexation and to serve the new State in the United States Senate.

Doubtless the persuasiveness of Sam Houston and his enthusiasm for the future of the country was of some influence in Rusk's decision to settle in Nacogdoches and stake his future in Texas. The exact date of his arrival in Texas has been the subject of some difference of opinion. However, a letter which he wrote to his wife establishes the time at about January 15, 1835. The first public record of his presence under the Mexican flag was made February 11, 1835, when he appeared before the Alcalde (mayor and judge) of Nacogdoches, Radford Berry, and took the oath of allegiance:

> "In the town of Nacogdoches, on the 11th day of February, 1835, before me Citizen Radford Berry, sole constitutional alcalde of this town and its municipality, and attesting witnesses, came and appeared the foreigner, Thomas J. Rusk who deposed upon oath, stated and declared that he is a native of the United States of North America; that his religion is Christian, his age twenty-nine years, his status married with a family, his occupation farming and stock-raising; that he desires to dwell under a wise and just government which offers the protection of its beneficent laws to honest and industrious men; and that he comes motivated by the invitation which this government extends to foreigners to come and settle within its terri-

[2]James, Marquis, The Raven, (cop. 1929 by Marquis James, 1956 by Jacqueline Mary Parsons James. By permission of the publishers, The Bobbs-Merrill Co.) p. 211. Hereafter referred to as Raven.

tory and as a friend of this country intending to loct here.

"To this end the oath to obey, support and defend the laws of this Country and the general and other laws of the State having been administered, he signed this act with me, the aforesaid alcalde and attesting witnesses according to the requirements of law."[4]

The document is signed by Rusk as principal, by the Alcalde, and witnessed by Sam Houston and Nat Robbins. Rusk's age, it will be noticed, was given at 29; actually he was 31. He may have been confused about his age; more likely it was simply a clerical error. He listed his occupation as "farming and stock-raising" as that was one of the enterprises he would follow. He could not practice law in a land in which he knew nothing of the laws or of the Spanish language. Formerly new settlers had been required to subscribe to the Catholic faith, but this requirement had been lifted in 1834. The die had been cast. The man who came to Texas on a fool's errand stayed to play a major role in the building of an empire.

Four days after taking the oath of allegiance to Mexico, Rusk wrote his wife, Mary Cleveland Rusk, in Clarksville, Georgia, announcing his decision to move to Texas and describing the new country and its opportunities in glowing terms:

"Nacogdoches, Texas 15th Feby. 1835

"Dear Mary—

"I again resume my pen to write you. I have been in this town about four weeks and have now seen enough of this Country to make up my mind to move to Texas and live. I prefer this part of the Country for several reasons. It is not as rich land as some other parts but taking it altogether it is better on account of health and good Society than any part of the whole Country. It will be in my opinion as healthy here as on the Blue ridge and the climate is much more mild and pleasant and the Society here is much better than in Clarksville. There are in this Town about Three hundred Americans and about two hundred Spaniards and the Country all around is settled up with Americans. The land is fine and the country affords all the conveniences and most of the luxuries of life and those who will be prudent and industrious here must become wealthy very soon. I have written you once before description of the Country and also have written a description of it to your Father. I have McLaughlin here waiting for

[4]Nacogdoches Archives, Texas State Library. (Translated from the Spanish.)

5

his brother who has his money and I shall not leave him until he pays me at least a part of what he owes me. That is the cause of my remaining here so long as I do not intend he shall slip through my fingers a second time—I have not heard of Smith or Buford."[5]

The reference here to McLaughlin, Smith and Buford apparently concerns the men accused of the "gold mine" swindle. The letter continues, expounding in glowing—perhaps gullible—terms the opportunities for making a quick fortune in Texas:

"I find the practice of Law here will be a pretty good business there being few in this Country that are talented. Governor Houston[6] lives in this place and has made over two Thousand Dollars in the last twelve months but he is very dissipated and in very bad health. The opening here I consider very good. I have a speculation on foot here which if I succeed at it will make me a fortune and if I fail I shall lose nothing. I have become well acquainted with some of the most distinguished men of the Country and they all profess great friendship and make many kind offers of their services to me and upon the whole I have taken a much better stand amongst them than I had any right to have expected so soon. I shall procure a tract of land in this neighborhood If I can which will answer Johnson, your Father and me and urge on them the importance of moving to this Country next Fall. I will try and have a years provisions laid up for all of us by fall—You must write me to Natchitoches, Louisiana from which place I can get your letters."[7]

In spite of his recent debacle in Georgia, Rusk already was stirred by dreams of riches in Texas. In compliance with the Mexican colonization law of 1825, he filed on May 23, 1835, a certificate of character and loyalty, signed by C. H. Sims, affirming that "the foreigner, Thomas J. Rusk, is a man of very good morality, habits and industry; lover of the Constitution and laws of the country and of the Christian religion; married, with family."[8]

---

[5]Thomas J. Rusk to Wife, Mary, February 15, 1835. Original in Rusk Papers, University of Texas Archives. The Rusk Papers comprise a large collection, assembled from various sources.
[6]Sam Houston had served as Governor of Tennessee—hence the title used here.
[7]Continuing letter to Mary, February 15, 1835, Rusk Papers, Rusk wrote entirely without punctuation. Essential marks have been added by the author.
[8]Nacogdoches Archives.

CHAPTER 2

Disciple of John C. Calhoun

As a native of South Carolina, Thomas J. Rusk brought with him to Texas a heritage of the frontiersmen with their zeal for liberty and resentment of restraint. He was born in the old Pendleton District in the "up Country" at the foothills of the Alleghenies on a plantation owned by the great Southern statesman, John C. Calhoun.

His father, John Rusk, was a late comer to the area, having arrived from Ireland in 1791. He settled in the Scotch-Irish Presbyterian community near the present town of Clemson—site of Clemson College. He was a stonemason by trade and soon established a reputation as a skillful builder. Some ten years after his arrival, he married Mary Starritt,[1] who came from an old established line of rugged pioneers.

Their first child, a son, was born December 5, 1803, during the first term of the Jefferson administration. The fond parents named him Thomas Jefferson Rusk for the democratic President whom they must have greatly admired.

If John and Mary Rusk had dreams that their son might emulate his great namesake, they were not too far beside the mark. In many respects, Rusk and Jefferson shared a common destiny—though who could conceive that the fame of Tom Rusk would be earned in a foreign land. The Declaration of Independence for the thirteen colonies had been written and adopted, but that for Texas was still to be drafted and signed. The American Revolution had been fought and won, but Texas' freedom was still to be achieved. Thomas Jefferson had filled the office of Secretary of State, but Rusk was to occupy the post of Secretary of War in a new nation to the southwest. Both spoke with wisdom in congressional halls; both took a hand in the westward expansion of the Anglo-American domain. Jefferson became President, but the presidency of the Texas Republic was twice

---

[1]The family name of Rusk's mother is found with some variations in spelling. "Starritt" is the form appearing in public records and family correspondence.

7

within the grasp of his distinguished namesake and was twice refused.

Rusk's boyhood was spent in an area wrested from the wilderness and the savages by rugged pioneers who subsequently lambasted the British and Tories in the War of Independence. The old Pendleton District embraced the present counties of Anderson, Oconee and Pickens, in the northwest corner of the State. It was an area in which the memories of the Revolution were fresh and its heroic deeds proudly cherished. While the father, John Rusk, had arrived after the conflict, many veterans of the war were leaders in the community, among them kinsmen on the Starritt side. "It was an age of high ideals, strong convictions and vigorous action. Its dominant political creed was 'Free Trade, State's Rights, Liberty or Death'."[2]

"It is probable that John Rusk resided first on the Fort Hill plantation which later became the home of John C. Calhoun, and is now the site of Clemson College," asserts R. T. Jaynes in his small book on the Rusk ancestry. "It is also probable that Thomas Jefferson Rusk was born on the Fort Hill plantation, but his boyhood home was on Cane creek near the town of Walhalla."[3] Other authorities concur that the family lived in a house belonging to Calhoun at the time of Tom's birth.

"John Rusk was honest, thrifty and an industrious worker. He was jovial, friendly and a splendid conversationalist," according to family tradition. "He greatly enjoyed an evening at the tavern with an interested and indulgent audience of his neighbors, who readily forgave a little over-indulgence in the brandy of which he was so fond."[4]

---

[2]Jaynes, R. T., **Thomas Jefferson Rusk,** (a small book, privately published, Walhalla, S. C., 1944) p. 7. Hereafter referred to as "Jaynes." This book-includes some reprints from sources other than the author, a South Carolina attorney.
[3]Ibid., p. 2
[4]Blount, Lois Foster, **A Brief History of Thomas J. Rusk Based on His Letters to His Brother, David, 1835-1856** in **Southwestern Historical Quarterly** ('Austin, 1931) Vol. 34, p. 188. This paper hereafter referred to as "Blount."
Mrs. Lois Fitzhugh Foster Blount, author of the article refered to, has carried on research on Rusk for many years and is due credit and appreciation for seeking out and helping to preserve many of the valuable materials which are included in the Rusk Papers in the University of Texas Archives. It was she who identified the socalled "El Paso Papers" which were procured by the University. She is also responsible for assembling some important Rusk materials in the Special Collection of the Stephen F. Austin State University Library. Mrs. Blount was born in Huntsville, Texas, May 24, 1896, and lived in San Marcos from 1903 to

John Rusk built the Old Stone Presbyterian Church, which, from the historical point of view, was his masterpiece. It was constructed in rectangular shape of durable rough-hewn stone and stands today, after 173 years, near the Clemson College campus, the former Calhoun plantation of Fort Hill. When he died in 1844, he was buried in the church cemetery. His grave was marked by a rough field stone for nearly a century until a granite monument was erected by the State of Texas in 1937, honoring him and his wife, Mary. Beneath the name of John Rusk on the double stone is the inscription, "Builder of the Old Stone Church." Below the dates of births and deaths of the couple are the lines: "Mother and Father of Thomas Jefferson Rusk, 1803-1857, Pioneer Soldier, Statesman of Texas."

Mary Starritt Rusk, Tom's mother, "was highly intelligent, notably pious, and . . . her son's education began at her knee with the Bible as a text book," according to Jaynes. The boy's formal schooling seems to have been limited to the little country school. Even there, according to a family anecdote, he was sometimes a reluctant pupil. He had been told that he could not come to school without his book. His path to school crossed a creek by a footbridge. By "chance" he dropped his book in the creek and figured then he could not go to school any more.[5]

Nevertheless, he learned in the country school to read, write and cipher, a foundation which opened the door to self-education and development of an excellent command of the English language as evinced in his speaking and writing of mature years.

Some writers have erroneously referred to Thomas J. Rusk's ancestry as "Irish." Even Sam Houston spoke of him as "my Irish friend." Actually he was Scotch-Irish—an important distinction. The native Irish were Catholic and, from the early 17th century were in conflict, often bloody war, with the Scottish and English Protestants of Northern Ireland, called Ulster— a bitter enmity that flares today after three and a half centuries.

1925. She received her B.A. degree from the University of Texas and the M.A. from Columbia University. In 1925, she married Guy Arthur Blount, grandson of Stephen William Blount, signer of the Texas Declaration of Independence, and veteran of the Texas Army. Her husband died in an automobile accident in 1937.

Mrs. Blount served for many years as an instructor in Stephen F. Austin State University and assisted in the Library. She lives in her lovely old home in Nacogdoches, built by her husband in 1908. There she continues her historical studies and writings.
[5]Ibid., p. 188.

During the 17th century, thousands of Scots of the Presbyterian faith settled in Northern Ireland and became known as the Ulster Scots. Then during the first half of the 18th century, as a result of religious and political persecution as well as economic depression, some 200,000 of these Ulster Scots flocked to the American Colonies. Because they were of Scottish ancestry but came from Ireland, they came to be called Scotch-Irish. They were almost universally of the Presbyterian faith.

Tough, courageous and resentful of restraint, the Scotch-Irish proved the best pioneers and the bravest fighters in American history. The British blamed them for starting the Revolution. Besides their valor in war, they supplied the nation with many of its greatest statesmen. Just as in the American Colonies, the Scotch-Irish had a major role as pioneers, soldiers and statesmen of Texas.

"It is reasonably certain that he [John Rusk] was Scotch-Irish because he came from Ireland as a patriot-refugee at a time when patriotic Protestants were needing to leave . . .," writes Judge R. W. Stayton.[6] The fact that he lived and married among the Scotch-Irish, built a Presbyterian church and was buried in a Presbyterian graveyard more definitely identifies him as Scotch-Irish. So was his wife, Mary Starritt, giving their son, Thomas J. Rusk, a double strain of the Scotch-Irish heritage, shared by John C. Calhoun, Sam Houston, David Crockett, James Bowie, Andrew Jackson, James Polk, Grover Cleveland and an imposing array of other presidents, warriors, statesmen and stalwart citizens of every walk of life.

Possibly the fact that he bore the name of Thomas Jefferson was a source of inspiration to Tom Rusk, the boy, to strive for greatness—though he probably never met Jefferson. It was John C. Calhoun who noticed the youth's ability and set him on the road of diligent study and hard work that eventually led to fame. It must have been admiration of Calhoun, his father's landlord, that stirred his ambition to be a lawyer. Calhoun loaned him books, helped him in his studies and got him a place in the district clerk's office where he could work and study law. At the same time young Rusk held a second job as part-time clerk in a grocery store. Soon after Calhoun

---

[6]Stayton, R. W., Address on Thomas J. Rusk before the Texas Bar Association, Published in **Texas Law Review,** (October Issue, 1925) p. 7. Hereafter referred to as "Stayton."

was elected Vice President of the United States in 1824, Rusk passed his examination for admission to the bar and moved across the line to Georgia to hang out his shingle. It would be many years before mentor and protege were closely associated again.

It was 1825 and Rusk was 22 years old when he began law practice in Clarksville, Habersham County, Georgia, not far from his old family home in South Carolina. In Clarksville, his uncle, Jehu Starritt lived, and the Starritts were among the leading citizens of the county. There Rusk soon built a successful and profitable practice. As a handsome young attorney, his social standing was such that he ventured to woo the daughter of one of the more prominent and wealthy families in town. He was married January 4, 1827, to Mary F. (Polly) Cleveland, daughter of General Benjamin Cleveland, merchant and landowner who served his county for 20 years in the Georgia Legislature.[7] Back in South Carolina, some of John Rusk's friends chided him about his son marrying "an aristocrat." The Clevelands were said to be of the same distinguished family into which President Grover Cleveland later was born.[8]

Now that Rusk had taken on the responsibilities of a family, he entered a partnership with his father-in-law in the merchandising business in addition to his extensive law practice. The first child was born to Tom and Mary Rusk February 24, 1828, and was named Benjamin Livingston. A second son, John Cleveland, came December 9, 1829, followed two years later by young Thomas Jefferson on January 12, 1832, and the fourth son, Cicero, was born October 5, 1834.

Then tragedy struck the heretofore happy family. The third son, Thomas Jefferson Rusk, Jr., died October 14, nine days after Cicero's birth. Almost at the same time, the crash came in Rusk's gold mining venture, leaving him financially ruined. In despondency over the death of his son and loss of his fortune as well as remorse for possibly having involved others in financial losses, he set out for Texas to hunt the swindlers. It was a time when he could not have faced his old friend and benefactor, John C. Calhoun, who having resigned the vice-presidency, was now a leader in the United States Senate.

---

[7] Jaynes, p. 33.
[8] **Ibid.**

11

CHAPTER 3

"Loud-Mouthed, Impatient Men"

Thomas J. Rusk barely had time to hang up his hat in Texas before he was involved in the political turmoil of the times. His new-found friend, Sam Houston, who himself had been naturalized as a citizen of the Mexican Republic only a few months before, was already engaged in political ventures. Rusk learned that the Anglo-American leaders were divided roughly into the "War Party" and the "Peace Party." Houston, at least publicly, leaned toward peace, believing the rank-and-file of Texas settlers were not ready for revolution.

Rusk was inclined to watch, listen and study the current situation before taking a stand. He probably would have preferred to attend to his own affairs of accumulating some of the rich Texas land which could be bought for fifty cents an acre, establishing himself as a farmer and stockraiser and eventually resuming the law practice which, for the time being, he must necessarily set aside.

However, it was not long before he was speaking his opinions and had his first brush with Mexican authorities. Later in life he could recount the incident with a sense of humor: "I remember that in 1835, shortly after I went to Texas, being at Nacogdoches, I was called on to attend one of these 'juntas' or conventions by the alcade," Rusk related in the United States Senate. "Certain questions were laid before us, and we were invited to express our opinion upon them. I expressed mine very freely; and, after the meeting was broken up, the alcalde ordered me to be taken to the calaboose; and if there had not been more Americans present than Mexicans, I should have been imprisoned for the expression of my opinion."[1]

In early 1835, the people of Texas, by and large, busy with their farms, ranches, stores and crafts, were apathetic amidst the political frenzy going on in the few scattered towns such as San Felipe, Brazoria, and to a milder extent, Nacog-

[1]Congressional Globe (Washington, D. C.) Dec. 18, 1848, XX, P. 48.

12

doches. The past two years had been difficult ones for the settlers, marked by crop-failures and a dreadful amount of sickness and death. To the usual plagues of chills, fever and pneumonia had been added in some areas outbreaks of Asian cholera.

However, during these same two years, there had been a breathing spell in the conflict with Mexican authorities which had been building up for a number of years. Mexico had won its independence from Spain in 1821 and thereafter adopted a Federal Constitution in 1824, a document which was to figure largely in the Texas revolt which had reached a high pitch by 1832.

Rusk learned that friction between the Anglo-American settlers and the Mexican government had been growing since the Congress in Mexico City passed the law of April 6, 1830, prohibiting further immigration of American settlers, except in two of the colonies. At the same time, in an effort to limit the growing trade with the United States, duties were imposed on all imports.

The Mexican Constitution of 1824, while generally liberal by Latin standards, had some provisions irksome to the Texas settlers, such as the requirement that all settlers be Catholics, and by the absence of such civil rights as the trial by jury and right of bail. But now, under a dictatorship in Mexico City, even this Constitution was revoked. This was cause for violent reaction and the Texans in petitions to the National Government demanded restoration of the Constitution of 1824 as the minimum relief.

In this tense situation, local armed skirmishes had occured, such as the Battle of Velasco, June 26, 1832, in which Texans captured the Mexican command, and at Anahuac, where a band of Texans attacked Mexican soldiers under Col. John D. Bradburn, a former American. The Texans involved in this Anahuac affair adopted what were known as the "Turtle Bayou Resolutions," declaring they were not in revolt against Mexico but were supporting the revolution of General Santa Anna (then considered a liberal) against the current dictator, President Bustamente.

Another encounter, the Battle of Nacogdoches, was still fresh on the minds of the people of the Redlands when Rusk arrived. He listened to their account of the battle there which occurred August 2, 1832, following on the heels of the fight at Anahuac.

The clash at Nacogdoches had erupted when Jose de las Piedras, commandant of the garrison under the Bustamente regime, ordered all residents to turn in their firearms. This was a challenge the people could not abide — imagine a Texan without a gun! The Ayuntamiento (town council), joined by the Spanish-speaking Alcalde, voted not to obey the order, and demanded that Piedras give his support to the cause of Santa Anna, against Bustamente.

When Piedras refused, the Redlands volunteers, under Col. James W. Bullock, attacked the Mexican garrison. After a fight in town, Piedras attempted to move his force to San Antonio but was intercepted by 17 determined Texas settlers and captured with his 400 men. In the two encounters, 33 Mexicans were killed and some 17 wounded. Of the Texans, three were killed and seven wounded. Among the Texan dead was the courageous Alcalde of Nacogdoches, Encarnacino Chirino.

Other encounters followed and by the end of the summer of 1832, every Mexican garrison had been driven out or withdrawn from Texas. Many Texans did not approve this resort to violence, but now that the acts had been done, all would be forced into the Revolution that was to follow after a comparatively quiet two years.

"It was rebellion, successful rebellion," writes Historian Herbert Gambrell, "but the complication of Mexican politics and the adroit work of Stephen F. Austin, who was still of the opinion that his 'standing motto—Fidelity to Mexico—ought to be on every man's mouth' . . . were to make it appear for a time as something else."[2]

For nearly a century (1727 to 1824) Texas was a separate province under Spain and then briefly under the new Republic of Mexico. But under an Act of the Mexican Congress in 1824, Texas was combined with Coahuila in a provisional State. However, there was a provision that *"so soon as Texas shall be in a condition to figure as a state of itself, it shall inform Congress thereof, for its resolution."*[3]

---

[2]Gambrell, Herbert, **Anson Jones, The Last President of Texas** (Annotated edition, University of Texas Press, Austin, 1964) p. 33.
[3]Yoakum, Henderson K., **History of Texas** (Redfield, New York, 1855) I, p. 469. Hereafter referred to as "Yoakum."

The Texans now fastened upon this clause. They were exceedingly unhappy with their forced union with Coahuila. As a very small minority, they could not bring about desired reforms in the joint State Legislature. Now, having driven the Mexican soldiers out of Texas, they were emboldened to ask for separate statehood under the provision of the Act of Congress in 1824. Accordingly, a convention for the purpose of drafting a proposed state constitution was called for October 1, 1832, in San Felipe. However, the absence of a number of delegates prevented conclusive action.

A second convention was held at San Felipe April 1, 1833. A proposed state constitution for Texas was drafted by a committee of which Sam Houston was chairman. Houston said it was the best constitution ever written. Someone has remarked that Houston should have known, as he wrote it himself. A memorial to the National Government, enumerating the problems of Texas and asking for separate statehood, drawn up by David G. Burnet, was adopted. Delegates selected to present the petition were Stephen F. Austin, William H. Wharton and J. B. Miller. As it turned out, Austin alone carried the proposals to Mexico City as the others were either unable or reluctant to make the trip.

Austin was one of the peace party. A dozen years before, he had gone to Mexico City and completed arrangements for his colony, which had since grown and prospered. This time he went with a "heavier heart" than he had gone on his former mission. ". . . before his Texas was filled with loud-mouthed, impatient men who had no way of knowing what sweat and toil and tears it had cost to bring the region to a point where they would want to take control of politics."[4]

Austin left for Mexico soon after the convention but on his arrival at the Mexican capital was kept cooling his heels while a struggle for power went on between Mexican leaders. Finally he received an audience and a promise that most of the grievances would be remedied. He started home in February, 1834, but was arrested en route because a letter he had written fell into the hands of authorities. He was thrown in a dungeon prison for four months and then detained in Mexico for a longer period. By that time Santa Anna had consolidated his dictatorship and sent Austin home with a promise

[4]Gambrell, Anson Jones, p. 35.

to grant the Texas petitions with the exception of that of separate statehood, which was the main point of contention.

It was early September, 1835, when Austin arrived home. He was now convinced that war was inevitable and he switched to the aggressive side. Meanwhile, Santa Anna had abolished the state government of Texas and Coahuila by dispersing the Congress, arresting the governor and setting up a figurehead. The fact that there was now no effective state government and there was grave danger of Indian ravages, gave ample reason for the program of organizing committees of public safety in the various municipalities which was now inaugurated under Austin's leadership.

CHAPTER 4

"We Will Not Speak in Forked Tongues"

Thomas J. Rusk, newest of the newcomers on the Texas scene—young, vigorous and personable—was readily accepted among the leaders of the resistance against Santa Anna's tyranny. He was cautious and reticent at first but before long was deeply involved in the turbulent political affairs which followed Austin's return to Texas.

Under the program of consultations in the various towns to organize committees of public safety, two emmisaries came to Nacogdoches. Houston and Rusk were among the leaders who were interviewed and both said the people of the East Texas area were not in favor of war-like measures—that they were "submissionists".[1] As a matter of fact, the older settlers in that area, as well as in other parts of the country, resented the militant activities of the newcomers and thought they should "keep their mouths shut."

Nevertheless, the war party emmisaries, Mosely Baker and F. W. Johnson, proceeded to San Augustine where they met with a warmer reception. It was only a few days before the people of Nacogdoches fell in line and joined in a meeting of representatives of the Redlands at San Augustine. Sam Houston offered a set of resolutions setting forth grievances which were adopted "unanimously"—with Rusk present but not voting. Apparently, he was still being deliberate in deciding his stand. The resolutions declared adherence to the Constitution of 1824, deplored evidences of tyranny, and declared there was now no legitimate head of the State Government.

"The resolutions further provided for negotiations with the Indian tribes, for raising and organizing the militia and for appointing a committee of safety. They also declared that those who should fly the country should forfeit their lands."[2]

---

[1]Wortham, Louis J., A History of Texas (Wortham-Molyneaux Co., Fort Worth, 1924) II, p. 279.
[2]Yoakum, I, p. 351.

17

Rusk served as secretary of a meeting in Nacogdoches July 19, 1835, when the local committee of vigilance and correspondence was formed. He had found a place where he was able to render his first great service for the people of Texas with whom he had cast his lot. He was assigned on the committee for negotiating peace and friendship with the Indians.

Semi-civilized tribes in the east and wild Indians in the west were becoming a serious threat to the white settlers, particularly if war should break out and they should be persuaded to join the Mexican side. According to Yoakum, " . . . there were more than a thousand warriors among the different tribes that had immigrated from the United States and almost surrounded the frontier of eastern Texas."[3]

As a member of the committee, Rusk wrote a protest against the admission of additional Indians from the United States. More effective, however, was his joint efforts with Sam Houston in negotiating with the tribal chiefs. Rusk and Houston were included on a deputation sent jointly by Nacogdoches and San Augustine. The Cherokees were disturbed by the fact that surveyors were coming into their territory, marking trees and establishing land claims.

In the course of their negotiations, a quaint letter was written jointly by Rusk and Houston to the Cherokee chiefs, addressed:

"Our Friends, Big Mush, Col. Bowles and the other Red Men, Brothers."

Worded in poetic "Indian talk", the letter dated September 24, 1835, assured the chiefs that their lands and people would be disturbed no further by the white men and added:

"The path that leads from one friends door to another should be open and bright friendship should make them hold each other by the hand. You say that your counsels are not dark and we believe you. That you may know that ours are not to be in darkness we invite you and others of your chiefs . . . as well as our Shawnee friends to attend our counsel on the Brasos where we will pay your expenses and treat you as friends and Brothers . . ." The reference was to the forthcoming Consultation at San Felipe.

The chiefs were further promised that "we will not speak

[3]Ibid., p. 358

18

in forked tongues but that we speak with one tongue only and walk in a straight path as long as the Trees bring forth leaves and so long as the rain shall fall on the Earth so long shall our words remain true."

The letter, signed in red by Thomas J. Rusk and Sam Houston, assured the Red Men that "White Men shall not trouble you by making marks on the trees on your lands. If they should attempt to do so, if you will inform the authorities they will be punished as the people wish at all times to meet our Red Brothers in peace and hold them by the hand forever. . . . We hope to see you when we set out to the Talk on the Brasos."[4]

As a result of the negotiations carried on by Rusk and Houston, peace was established with the Indians—a truce which for the most part was observed throughout the period of the Revolution. It was a great asset to the colonists and, for the time being, left the Indians undisturbed on the lands they occupied.

*   *   *   *

After committees of public safety had been organized in districts throughout Texas under Austin's plan, a General Consultation was announced to convene in San Felipe in November. But before that time arrived, guns blazed and blood was shed in the Battle of Gonzales, an encounter referred to as "the Lexington of Texas." The people of Gonzales owned a small cannon which the Mexican authorities decided to confiscate, but Texas volunteers placed a sign beside the weapon, reading "Come and Take It." In the sharp fight which ensued, the Mexican force was sent scurrying back to San Antonio.

The shedding of blood after two years of comparative quiet, aroused the population throughout Texas. In the Nacogdoches district, where the people had leaned hopefully toward peace, a meeting was called at San Augustine. There Thomas J. Rusk mounted the platform to deliver what might be termed his "maiden speech" in Texas, where his oratory was to become noteworthy.

He aroused his audience to fever pitch with "an eloquent appeal to their patriotism." Putting words into action he de-

[4]**Papers of Mirabeau Bonaparte Lamar,** Texas State Library, Ed. Charles Adams Gulick, Jr., I, p. 239. Referred to hereafter as "Lamar Papers."

clared: "I will be one of a volunteer company to march at once to the rescue of our living countrymen and the avenging of the slain!" As one writer remarked, "The enthusiastic response of the crowd before him, was evidence enough that the youthful stranger had found the way through their rough and tough exteriors into their warm hearts."[5]

"From that time until the day of his death, Thomas Jefferson Rusk was a Texian in every just and honorable sense of the word," spoke Chief Justice John Hemphill years later, looking back upon Rusk's distinguished career.[6] It was not a passing flash of emotional response. From that time on Rusk was not only a Texian but a recognized leader in the affairs of the country.

A company of volunteers was organized on the spot and Rusk was chosen to lead it to the scene of war. After a few days of training and drill, the company was ordered to San Antonio de Bexar where the Texans were laying siege to the town. The object, according to a circular issued throughout the province, was "to take Bexar and drive the Mexican soldiery out of Texas." But Rusk was not to lead his company for there was need for him in higher ranks. The Nacogdoches unit was scheduled to leave for the scene of war October 10. In compliance with General Austin's orders, the Redlands militia made a noisy display with blaring bugles and rolling drums on their arrival at San Antonio in order to impress the enemy inside their fortifications.

Rusk had arrived at the war front ahead of the troops. Instead of commanding the Nacogdoches company, he was immediately pressed into service by General Austin as commander of the Fourth Cavalry. Totally inexperienced in warfare as he was, one can imagine his trepidations when he was assigned a highly dangerous mission. The Mexicans were entrenched in the city and a strategy was developed to draw them out of their walls. In a daring attempt, Rusk, with forty horsemen, rode out from the Texans' lines and took up a position in the open, only 300 feet from the enemy works and remained there for 20 minutes, "but the defenders would not come out to this human bait and did not even strike at it."[7]

[5]Texas Almanac Compendium, p. 60.
[6]Hemphill, John, Chief Justice of Texas Supreme Court, Eulogy in Texas House of Representatives, from copy in Stephen F. Austin State University Library, Hereafter referred to as "Hemphill".
[7]Yoakum, II, p. 17.

CHAPTER 5

Rusk and Austin: "There Was a Tie Between Them"

In the battle near San Antonio, known as the "Grass Fight," Thomas J. Rusk was under enemy fire for the first time and acquitted himself with valor. At some later date, he wrote an eye-witness account of the battle. He makes no mention of the legend that the Mexican detachment with a string of burros with bags on their backs were believed by the Texans to be carrying silver for the enemy's payroll. He does record the fact that the famous Texas spy, Deaf Smith, mistook the party for enemy reinforcements which had been expected from Laredo. According to Rusk's account:

> "Deaf Smith had been for some days on the look out in the direction of Laredo, and on the morning of the 26th [of November, 1835] he was seen coming across the field at full speed making his way to headquarters, he . . . stated that a body of Mexicans which he supposed was the reinforcement were about five miles west of Town [San Antonio] and coming in. General Burleson ordered out about forty cavalry under the command of Col [James] Bowie to intercept and delay them until about one hundred and seventy infantry which he ordered out could come up. Smith said he thought the Mexican force was about five hundred. . . . Bowie dashed on with his horseman and intercepted the enemy about a mile from town and about four miles from our camp. It turned out to be about one hundred & fifty Mexican cavalry who had been sent out of town for the purpose of procuring grass for their horses. Bowie immediately commenced an attack."[1]

Meanwhile, the Texan infantry arrived on the field and Rusk was included in the force which dashed to the relief of James Bowie. The Texans came unexpectedly under heavy fire and were thrown into confusion but continued fighting.

---

[1]Rusk Papers, University of Texas Archives.

"Our forces by this time were scattered over about one hundred acres of ground & in small parties, every man fighting pretty much on his own hook," Rusk reported. "We however kept advancing on the enemy and they falling back. We got in about Eighty yards of the Cannon when it was discharged on us with grape & canister and run back a short distance when they halted & fired again." The bitterest part of the battle followed:

> ". . . they then attempted to charge with I think about a hundred and fifty cavalry on about forty of our men who were occupying a little eminence on the field to prevent the enemy bringing their cannon to that point which would have given them advantage. The cavalry came up at a beautiful charge until they got within about one hundred yards when they broke their ranks and fell back. They twice repeated this attempt of a charge but failed to get any nearer us than about hundred yards. About this time Morales Battalion was brought up to drive our men from the eminence. These men advance with great coolness and bravery under a destructive fire from our men, preserving all the time strict order and exhibiting no confusion, they got up in about twenty yards of our position. All our guns and pistols had been fired off & we had no time to reload & must have tried the butts of our guns against their Bayonets but for the fact that some of our men who were fighting in a different place hearing the steady fire . . . attempted to come to them and in coming across the field ran nearly upon the enemys cannon. The Mexicans took it for granted that it was an attempt to take their cannon. They soon after retreated until they came under cover of the Guns of the Town."[2]

In his account of the battle, Rusk recalled a minor incident of war: "a little boy was setting down behind a bunch of small bushes loading his gun. The Cannon was fired, and the whole charge of grape and Cannister struck the bushes & tore them literally to pieces, but the boy escaped unhurt." The fight had lasted about an hour and a half. The enemy dead was variously estimated "from forty to upwards of a hundred—I think the latter the more accurate. They carried off during the engagement a number of their dead, as I saw myself several dead men carried off on horseback during the fight."

Though the bags carried on the backs of the burros were filled with grass rather than silver, other materials were cap-

---

[2]Ibid.

tured and the total booty was sold and brought between "two & three thousand dollars." Casualties on the Texans' side were remarkably small. "We had four men slightly wounded and one of our men ran away and was never heard of until we got to Gonzales about seventy five miles," Rusk recounted.[3]

General Edward Burleson's official report of the battle mentions that "during the action it was ascertained that a party of Mexicans consisting of forty or fifty were firing on a party with Col. Johnson from cover; Col. Rusk discovering them called out for a party to charge on them and rout them, he made the charge with about fifteen men & routed them from their cover."[4]

With usual enthusiasm and thoroughness, Rusk was active in other phases of the Bexar Campaign. When morale was low due to inactivity, and suffering, he made "a short but pathetic & spirited address" to the army, urging the importance of keeping up the seige. William H. Jack also spoke and volunteers to remain in the service were called for. Some 400 responded, assuring eventual success.[5]

Rusk had been promoted to Colonel and assigned by General Austin as his aide-de-camp. The special assignment was of short duration as Austin was appointed as one of the commissioners to the United States to seek American aid. General Burleson was elected by the soldiers to take command.

Rusk now took the liberty of advising the Provisional Government that success of the campaign at San Antonio demanded supplies and reinforcements. As a result of this appeal, he was invited to appear before the Provisional Government at San Felipe to present his views. As the outcome, he was appointed by Governor Henry Smith and the Council to "proceed east of the Trinity to procure reinforcements and supplies for the besiegers, with power to press such as were deemed necessary, if not otherwise obtainable." Although San Antonio fell to the Texans "before these wise provisions could be carried out, the valuable assistance collected by Rusk, in men and munitions of war, were of great service to the Army in succeeding events."[6] In the course of his duties, Rusk called upon his home town of

[2]Ibid.
[4]Binkley, William C., Ed. **Correspondence of the Texas Revolution**, I, p. 126.
[5]**Ibid.**, I p. 142.
[6]Texas Almanac Compendium, p. 61.

Nacogdoches for $1,000 from the "public funds", which was promptly provided.

The war had developed so suddenly and the leaders of Texas were so busy fighting the enemy that it had been difficult to organize more than a semblance of State government. Many of the delegates who had been elected to the General Consultation in San Felipe failed to arrive. Hence, a loose organization that was called the "Permanent Council" served as the State government for three weeks until the General Consultation was organized November 2, 1835. At that time a constitution was adopted and a provisional State government set up with Henry Smith of Brazoria as Governor and James W. Robinson of Nacogdoches as Lieutenant Governor.

Sam Houston was elected commander-in-chief of the army and adopted a policy of recruiting, organizing and training a regular army, rather than the bold, precipitous action to which the Texas pioneers were inclined. He gave little attention to the siege of San Antonio, but "Old Ben" Milam led a heroic attack on the walls which forced General Cos to surrender with his 1400 men, though Milam was killed in the battle. Cos and his soldiers were granted parole to return to Mexico with the agreement not to bear arms again against Texas—a pledge that was soon broken. The victory left Texas once more free of all Mexican forces and the people were jubilant over their victories —but the wise ones knew that the foe would be back.

San Antonio fell to the Texans on December 9, the same day that Colonel Rusk left San Felipe for his recruiting assignment in East Texas. En route to Nacogdoches, Rusk received a letter from Barrett Royal, dated December 15, announcing the victory and reporting the death of Milam. There was also a letter of the same date from James W. Robinson, Lieutenant Governor and ex-officio President of the General Council, conveying the same information.[7]

Colonel Rusk was appointed Inspector General of the Army on December 14 and served in that capacity until February 26, 1836.[8] However, he continued his recruiting work, apparently filling both offices at the same time.

Rusk and Stephen F. Austin were never intimate friends but between them there was mutual admiration and respect.

---

[7]Rusk Papers.
[8]Kemp, Louis Wiltz, **The Signers of the Texas Declaration of Independence** (The Anson Jones Press, Salado, Texas, 1944) p. 307.

Neither was by nature or inclination a military man, but each recognized the ability and sincerety of the other in the task to be done. Both were modest and unselfish in their services for the cause of freedom. As one writer expressed it, "There was a tie between them. Colonl Rusk afterwards stated that Austin was the purest patriot and best man he had ever known."[9]

Though Austin had announced on his return from captivity in Mexico that war was the only solution, he still hesitated about a declaration of independence. After leaving San Antonio on his mission to the United States, he expressed his views, before embarking, in a letter to Rusk dated Quintana, December 25, 1835. In it, he warned against the political intriguers, "such as Wharton," and said "substantial farmers, proprietors and men of families must look into matters of their cwn rights as citizens."[10]

However, the enthusiastic reception which Austin was accorded in New Orleans convinced him that the time was ripe for independence. He wrote Rusk from that city, January 7, 1836: "You will perceive by the letter I wrote you from the mouth of the Brazos, that I was not in favor of precipitate measures. Since my arrival here, the information I have received has placed the subject in a different light—we can get all the aid, and support we need to sustain our independence, and even to take the war if necessary into the heart of Mexico. . . . There was a very large meeting last night of the citizens of N. O. in favor of Texas—it was enthusiastic in the extreme.

"I conclude by giving it as my opinion, (So far as at present inform'd) that we ought to declare independence when the convention meets—You are at liberty to inform your neighbors of my opinion on this subject—Respectfully your friend & Obt Sevt—S. F. Austin."[11]

[9]Stayton, p. 9.
[10]Rusk Papers, Austin to Rusk, Dec. 25, 1835.
[11]Ibid., Jan. 7, 1836.

CHAPTER 6

Hue and Cry in Habersham

While Rusk had been establishing himself in Texas, there was a bitter clamor in the old hometown of Clarksville back in Georgia. Rusk was not the only one who had suffered loss in the collapse of the mining and land promotion enterprise. General Benjamin Cleveland, Rusk's father-in-law, was a heavy loser. Leander Smith, a brother-in-law, was in financial trouble. Others outside the fimily were involved.

The courts of Habersham County were busy with suits, counter-suits and foreclosures. Thomas J. Rusk was made defendant in suits for his own debts as well as some for Leander Smith for obligations he had endorsed. Of course there were neighbors, relatives and clients who owed accounts and notes to Rusk, but few were able or willing to pay.

Rusk had left these accounts with his faithful young brother, David, only 19, who bore the brunt of abuse from all sides. David made diligent efforts to collect accounts and defend the name of his brother whom some were now branding with the epithet, "gone to Texas." With typically poor English and spelling, but with forthright expression, David scrawled a letter to his brother, Tom, on April 29, 1835:

> "Dear Brother I again Wright you but have nothing good to right you Habersham Court was Last weak There was a great many calls for you as well as I could learn several cases went aginst you and as for my part I was garnished in Several cases for your effects but did not answer to any of them Gnl Cleveland is intirly and finly broke up he has bin haild on Same a/c your debts the people hear are making great hugh and cry about you all most every person pretends to have claims against you and as for your Notes I have them and has made all the Executions to collect them and I find it impossible to collect any mony on your business I have collected a few Dollars along Enough to pay our expenses I have tryed in every way to collect money and almost every effort fails."[1]

---

[1]Rusk Papers, Univ. of Texas Archives, David to Thos. J. Rusk, Apr. 29, 1835.

26

The letter continued with reports of collection efforts on various accounts then turns to the matter of Rusk's family: "I want you to right to me when you want your family brought to you and how you think I had better cum as Polly [Mrs. Rusk] is anxious to cum to you and seems to be varry uneasy about cuming to you She thinks we will never get means enough to cum to you But you need not be the least uneasy about that yourself all the danger in it will be to get off from hear as they will be watching and will try to attach to stop us as the predudise is so against you."[2]

As if these difficulties were not enough, David adds, "The people hear believe you Smith McLaughlin Patton and Smith was all in copartnership in the hole transaction."[3] It was a reference to the gold mine debacle.

Thomas J. Rusk was anxious to have his wife, Polly, and the children with him as soon as he considered it safe for them in Texas. Letters which he wrote to his wife at this time are not available, but one which he directed to David, August 12, 1835, has been preserved. In it he gave legal advice concerning garnishments which had been served on David "as I do not wish Judgment to go against you." He spoke of preparations for bringing the family to Texas. "Let me know how you have succeeded, what amount you or Polly will have towards paying expenses &c. I want you all to be ready to start out here in December as I do not think it safe to start sooner. I have written Polly this day—"[4]

But David was not to have the responsibility of escorting the family to Nacogdoches. A hassle arose between him and Mrs. Rusk's family. Seemingly, the Clevelands were resentful of actions of Tom and expended some of their ire on his brother. Naturally, they might also feel that David was not mature enough to handle the responsibility of conducting Polly and the children on the long journey to Texas.

Anyway, there was a letter dated Jacksonville, Benton County, Ala., November 18, 1835, in which David complained of being "run over" and abused by the Clevelands and their son-in-law, Leander Smith. He never liked Smith. General and Mrs. Cleveland had been saying that Tom spent all they had given

²Ibid.
³Ibid.
⁴Blount, Thos. J. to David Rusk, Aug. 12, 1835.

to Polly and if he would not support his family Leander Smith could.[5] (As it turned out in later years, it was Rusk who supported Smith's family.)

Polly had been torn between affection for her parents and loyalty to her absent husband whom she was determined to join in Texas. She set out in early November, 1835, with her three children, accompanied by Leander Smith and presumably his wife, Ann—Polly's sister. They arrived in Nacogdoches about December 23. Disgruntled David made the trip alone and arrived in San Augustine about the same time. Tom sent for him to come to Nacogdoches December 23.[6]

Christmas, 1835, found the Rusk family united after a year of separation. Mary (Polly) Rusk rested from tension and weariness under the protection and love of her husband after the rugged overland journey which had required some six weeks. During a lull in Texas' stormy affairs, Tom Rusk could relax briefly and enjoy his family after a year of stress and loneliness. He could bask in fatherly pride with the three little boys, Benjamin, John and Cicero, who had grown amazingly during the twelve months. Brother David was there, too, looking taller at 19, eager to get into the war—a matter which was not long delayed.

Rusk had considered it unsafe to bring his family to Texas when he first arrived due to the turbulent situation and prevailing diseases. The health situation was now somewhat improved, but as to the general turmoil, the family's arrival came at the most perilous time in Texas history. The holiday interlude passed quickly as Rusk was called back to serve his adopted country in a new crises. Domestic life must wait.

Though the Mexican forces had been driven out of Texas in the short period of war in 1835, intelligence reports now said Santa Anna was assembling troops whom he personally would lead to Texas in March to crush the rebellion.

The state Provisional Government was deadlocked by disagreement between Governor Smith and the Council. The junta had been organized as a ruling body for a separate state in the Mexican Republic, but Governor Smith and some others were now demanding complete independence. The government became almost totally ineffective due to these differences and

---

[5]Rusk Papers, David to Thos. J. Rusk, Nov. 18, 1835.
[6]Ibid., Thos. J. to David, Rusk, Dec. 23, 1835.

steps had to be taken at once to save the fruits of victories that had been won on the battlefields.

Early in January, 1836, the Provisional Government called for a convention to meet in the town of Washington-on-the-Brazos on March 1. Election of delegates from the various districts was set for February 1.

CHAPTER 7

Rusk at Birth of New Republic

There was great commotion in Nacogdoches on election day, Monday, February 1, 1836. The polls were opened in the Old Stone Fort for the election of delegates to the Convention which had been called by the Provisional Government to meet in Washington-on-the-Brazos on March 1. Lines were tightly drawn between the faction favoring immediate independence from Mexico and the conservative side who supported the Mexican Constitution of 1824. The issue simply stated was "war or peace."

A company of volunteers which had just arrived from Newport, Ky., had been detained in town to vote for the independence side. The constitutionalists had enlisted on their side all the Mexican residents. The judges ruled that the soldiers, having just arrived in Texas, were not eligible to vote. There was an angry confrontation. The scene was described by William F. Gray of Virginia, who had just arrived in town the day before:

"The company was drawn up with loaded rifles, and the First Lieutenant, Woods, swore that the men would vote, or he would riddle the door of the Stone House, where the election was held, with rifle balls. The Captain, who had only arrived the night before, had not yet resumed command . . . and determined not to interfere, but to let the company and the judges fight it out. The citizens were then called on by a count of heads to decide whether the volunteers should vote or not, and the Constitutionalists outvoted the Independents some thirty votes. On this the Mexicans set up a shout of triumph, which enraged the volunteers, and it was feared they would fire on the citizens."[1]

However, there were speeches instead of gunfire and bloodshed. After some debate by others, Colonel Rusk, who was one of

---

[1]Gray, Col. Wm. F., Diary of, **From Virginia to Texas, 1835** (Gray, Dillaye & Co., Houston, 1909) p. 90.

the candidates on the constitutional side appeared in the role of peacemaker, a part which he was to play in many a controversy in his lifetime. He addressed the crowd and the volunteers, pleading for order, and announced that the judges were reconsidering their ruling and would announce their decision "after dinner." In the afternoon, the judges ruled that the volunteers could vote if they so desired. By that time, the soldiers had cooled off and resolved they would not vote. However, they soon changed their minds again and all voted.[2]

"They were all day under arms and frequently marched to and fro, with drum and fife, before the door of the Hustings—a shameful spectacle," Gray remarked. The voting continued next day and the angry feelings subsided. Even Gray, who had arrived on Sunday, cast his vote on Tuesday.

When the votes for the entire district were counted, Thomas J. Rusk, who had been in Texas only a year, led all others. He was launched on an illustrious political career. He received 392 votes of the 610 cast. The three other delegates elected were John S. Roberts, 263 votes; Charles S. Taylor, 258, and Robert Potter, 235.[3]

Before the Kentucky volunteers left town, Rusk again served as peacemaker. The citizens had lined up to bid the soldiers farewell. "They were treated with liquor, and some gents drank toasts in the street," Gray recorded. "Mr. J. K. Allen's toast gave offense to Mr. Potter, who resented it. Some sharp words were exchanged, and a fracas was about to ensue, which was prevented by the prompt interference of Col. Rusk, who rebuked and silenced them."[4]

Robert Potter was described by Colonel Gray as being regarded as a "disorganizer" who "can only float in troubled water." Rusk found it necessary to squelch him in the course of the Convention to which both had been elected. He was described by Reuben M. Potter (not related) as one in whom "unusual powers of brain and tongue were perverted by evil impulses . . . one of the most pestilent disturbers of the Washington-on-the-Brazos convention. His disorganizing propensities proved a serious bar to business until Rusk checked him in the only way, which with him [Potter] was effective. . . ."[5] The

[2]**Ibid.**
[3]Kemp, p. 308
[4]Gray, p. 90.
[5]Tolbert, Frank X., in **Dallas Morning News**, Oct. 25, 1965.

particular method is not specified. However, it may be taken into account that Rusk, though a man of peace, was physically powerful and wholly fearless.

All the heat generated in the election between the "independents" and the "constitutionalists" apparently was wasted as by the time the delegates arrived in Washington, all had switched to the "war party." Mexican soldiers already were back on Texas soil—ahead of schedule. The business at hand must be completed in great haste. All was confusion and much of the populace from the west was fleeing before the invasion. The vanguard of the flight, known as "the Runaway Scrape," was arriving in the town and some of the local residents were joining in the stampede when Rusk reached the scene.

The town of Washington itself was described by Colonel Gray as a "disgusting place." "About a dozen cabins or shanties constitute the city; not one decent house in it, and only one well-defined street, which consists of an opening cut out of the woods. The stumps still standing."[6]

The Convention of 1836 wasted no time in getting down to business. It was quickly organized in an unheated shed, though a norther had blown in, lowering the temperature to near freezing. In spite of the cold, delegates worked all night and came up next day, March 2, with a Declaration of Independence. The document recited the series of events which had brought the people of Texas to this critical juncture, and avowed:

> "In such a crisis, the first law of nature, the right of self-preservation—inherent and inalianable right of the people to appeal to first principles and take their political affairs into their own hands in extreme cases—enjoins it as a right toward themselves and a sacred obligation to their posterity to abolish such government and create another in its stead, calculated to rescue them from impending dangers, and to insure their future welfare and happiness."[7]

A long list of grievances is enumerated and it is then proclaimed to the world that the people "do hereby resolve and declare that our political connection with the Mexican nation has forever ended; and that the people of Texas do now constitute a free, sovereign and independent republic . . ."

[6]Gray.
[7]Excerpt from **Texas Declaration of Independence.**

32

The Declaration was unanimously adopted and signed by the delegates, including Thomas J. Rusk, now 33 years old. The average age of the signers was under 38. Most of the delegates were natives of the United States. Only two were of Texas origin.

The Convention then knuckled down to the task of writing a Constitution for the new Republic of Texas. Rusk was not a member of the committee charged with writing the document but, with his legal experience, gave valuable advice and assistance. After the charter was adopted, he was assigned the responsibility of putting the hurriedly-written document in proper form.

The historian, Eugene C. Barker, comments that Rusk had not had as much experience in public affairs as a number of the other men in the group, "but was evidently recognized as a man of superior ability and the record indicates that he took a keen interest in every issue that was raised. As chairman of the select committee to correct errors and phraseology in the final draft," Barker said that Rusk "may be regarded as being more responsible than any other man for the final wording of that instrument."[8]

As further appraisal, Barker adds: "The notable service Rusk later rendered as Chief Justice of the Supreme Court of the Republic of Texas and still later as United States Senator from Texas is evidence of his extraordinary ability, and explains the influence he wielded over the members."[9] In 17 days and nights, the historical Convention hammered out a Constitution that served the Republic well throughout its ten-year existence.

During the Convention, Rusk was a stickler for orderly procedure and impatient of any delay. Besides squelching Potter, as before mentioned, he brought his influence to bear in other occasions. Even the erudite Dr. Lorenzo de Zavala received a mild rebuke. The scholarly Mexican national, turned Texas patriot, was given to lengthy literary examples. Once when he began a speech with the words, "A Roman philosopher once said . . ." Rusk interrupted: "Dr. Zavala, I should like to hear sometime when I have more leisure what that Roman philosopher said. Right now though, we'd better be concerned with the living enemy rather than dead philosophers so we can

---

[8]Barker, Eugene C., **Texas History** (Southwest Press, Dallas, 1929) pp. 248-49.
[9]**Ibid.,** p. 249.

finish our work here in time for a good sleep before we have to run." Dr. Zavala graciously agreed.[10]

The new government was completed with the election of officers of the Republic. David G. Burnet was elected President. Dr. Zavala, who had become disenchanted with Santa Anna's dictatorial policies in Mexico and espoused the Texas cause, was named Vice-President. Cabinet members included Bailey Hardeman, Secretary of Treasury; Robert Potter, Secretary of Navy; David Thomas, Attorney General, and Samuel P. Carson, Secretary of State.

But by far, the most outstanding member of the Cabinet was Thomas J. Rusk, who was elected Secretary of War. It was a post that required wisdom, patience and diplomacy in a rowdy country where a weak government and rebellious army were constantly at odds. Rusk proved to be the sturdy link that held the shaky apparatus together until the war was won. As an example of Colonel Rusk's "unremitting toil and energetic action for Texas in her day of extremity," O. M. Roberts, who later became Governor of the State, is credited with a story:

> "The night after the organization of the government ad interim under Burnet a council was held. Burnet, in a dignified manner, called on one after another for an expression of opinion, coming last to Secretary of War Rusk, who, with his elbows on his knees and his head resting in his hands as if meditating, was actually fast asleep, as he had been at work night and day for three days on the Constitution. Punched in the ribs by the gentleman next to him, he brought himself to the perpendicular and said: 'I think we are in a hell of a fix. We are worked down. Let's go over to the saloon and get a drink, then mount our horses, and go and fight like the devil to get out of it'."[11]

Most of the members of the government did depart at once, some to the army, some to look after their families. Rusk remained with President Burnet a few days, rounding up the official records, after which they moved the seat of government to Harrisburg, with the approaching Mexican army at their heels. There Rusk carried on the pressing duties of his office for a short time before moving his post of action to the retreating Texas army.

Sam Houston had again been elected Commander-in-Chief

[10]Tolbert, Frank X., in **Dallas Morning News**, Oct. 25, 1965.
[11]Lubbock, Francis R., **Six Decades in Texas** (Austin, 1900) pp. 82-83.

34

and, while the Convention was still in session, departed to take command of the meager forces. With Santa Anna and his army of 5,000 troops sweeping through Texas like a prairie fire, there was nothing to do but order a strategic retreat. Houston's orders to William B. Travis, commanding the garrison of the Alamo in San Antonio, to destroy the fortification and move eastward, was not carried out. Instead, the fortress had been re-garrisoned and plans made by Travis and James Bowie to hold it at all costs. After a last heroic stand against the bloody assault on Sunday, March 6, the Alamo fell, only after every soldier of the garrison of some 189 men had died fighting.

Houston had left the Convention at Washington March 6, the day the Alamo fell, but was not aware of the disaster until he arrived in Gonzales March 11 to take command of the army. He had previously ordered James W. Fannin, who commanded a force at Goliad, to reinforce the garrison at the Alamo. Now he countermanded the order and instructed Fannin to fall back to Victoria as soon as practical. However, Fannin was delayed in carrying out the order and was trapped by General Jose Urrea with superior forces and, after a brave stand, surrendered his contingent of 300 men. Though the terms of surrender provided that the men were to be treated as prisoners of war, General Santa Anna personally ordered their execution in the infamous Goliad Massacre on Palm Sunday, March 27.

Houston halted his retreat temporarily at the Colorado River, where he held his troops for two days on the west side of the stream at Burnham's Crossing, then moved over to the east side and marched downstream to Beason's Ford. The pursuing enemy forces under General Sesma camped on the west side of the river, and the two armies remained there on opposite sides of the stream for five days. Here Houston had declared he would make a stand and his men were eager to fight. But the Commander-in-Chief suddenly changed his mind and resumed the retreat eastward toward the Brazos River.

There was much dissension in the army, the civilian population was panicking and the Government was alarmed and outraged. By the time the army reached the Brazos, its number was greatly reduced as many of the men had taken off, either with or without permission, some to take care of their families in the flight from the advancing Mexican armies. Arriving on March 31 at a point called Groce's, the Texas army encamped for nearly two weeks of reorganization, training and recruiting.

CHAPTER 8

Time to Bring the Enemy to Battle

While the Texas Army was camped on the west side of the Brazos, a tall man appeared on the east side of the stream and signaled that he wished to cross. Word was carried to General Houston who, probably expecting a new recruit, sent a negro across in a rowboat to bring over the "stranger." Thus the Secretary of War, Thomas J. Rusk, arrived on a difficult mission. He was warmly welcomed by his good friend, the Commander-in-Chief, who must have suspected the purpose of the visit.

Houston had been firing dispatches to President Burnet and Secretary Rusk, asking for supplies and equipment and lamenting the fact that the Government had moved from Washington-on-the-Brazos eastward to Harrisburg, thus contributing to the stampede of the populace. He was overlooking the matter of his own so-called Fabian retreat which was another prime cause of the panic.

Rusk had not been neglectful in his duties of supplying materials of war. He was "untiring in his efforts to forward supplies of all kinds. At the ferry at Washington, he stationed an officer with orders to let no one pass eastward who had a rifle and to take by impressment and forward to the Army all the powder, lead and horses he could."[1]

Rusk now had a delicate mission to perform—to carry out the orders of his Government to stop the retreat and, at the same time, avoid antagonizing his headstrong friend which might bring disaster to the whole cause. When Rusk was elected Secretary of War, General Houston had written his "young Irish friend," congratulating him on his advancement and assuring him that he would find in the Commander-in-Chief "a worthy subaltern."[2] This was a time for the General to make

[1]Yoakum, II, p. 111.
[2]Williams, Amelia W. and Barker, Eugene C., Eds. **The Writings of Sam Houston, 1813-1863** (University of Texas Press, Austin, 1938) I, p. 380. Hereafter referred to as "Houston's **Writings.**"

good on his lightly-given promise. He proved as good as his word.

The Government, headed by President Burnet, had ordered the Secretary of War to go to General Houston and to see that he retreated no further but began a campaign against the enemy.[3]

During the years which followed the war, much political controversy arose over details of the San Jacinto campaign and the final battle. President Burnet, in his account of events, quoted a letter by Col. William Austin, reading: "Col. Rusk was therefore ordered to repair to the headquarters of the army, and to compel it to take up a position before the enemy and bring him to battle at the first favorable position possible. . . . The President . . . stated that Col. Rusk was then being sent to the field with authority to take charge of the command of the army, if necessary to carry out the policy . . ."[4]

In a further effort to goad General Houston into action, President Burnet wrote to the commander: "The enemy are laughing you to scorn. You must fight them. You must retreat no farther. The country expects you to fight."[5]

Regardless of all the furor, Rusk received a cordial welcome and "remained in camp with Houston on the terms of the closest intimacy."[6] Houston wrote to their mutual friend, Henry Raguet, in Nacogdoches: "Col. Rusk is here, and from his presence, I hope for the best results and am well satisfied he will see the crisis over! He proves himself a Patriot and a soldier! There is the most perfect harmony in camp. Let his Lady know that he is in fine health & spirits. And says his presentiment is as good as he would wish. He says 'Victory and Independence'!"[7]

The Secretary of War and the Commander-in-Chief talked over the military situation. Houston explained his strategy and Rusk expressed the views of the Cabinet and the people in general. After the latest dispatches were in, reporting Santa Anna's movements, Houston remarked to Rusk: "We need not

---

[3]Wortham, III, p. 283.
[4]Barker, Eugene C., The San Jacinto Campaign in Texas State Historical Association Quarterly (Austin, April, 1901) Vol. IV, p. 330.
[5]Burnet to Houston from Harrisburg, April, 1836.
[6]Wortham, III, p. 283.
[7]Houston's Writings, I, p. 400.

talk. You think we ought to fight and I do too." Rusk nodded gravely.

Historians disagree as to whether Houston had planned to make a stand at the Brazos or intended to continue his retreat to Nacogdoches, or even to the United States border with the hope of eliciting American aid. Most of his biographers contend that he had no scheme for further retreat. However, he might have kept that alternative in mind as a last resort. He had vowed to fight until the Mexican armies were driven from Texas, even if he were forced to retreat to the Sabine—there to regroup and fight again. This was an expression of determination, rather that a stated plan.

From the time of Rusk's arrival in camp on April 4, there was in effect something in the nature of a joint command. Rusk was recognized as the superior authority while Houston was in command of the army and responsible for military tactics. Houston outlined his strategy, which involved some further delay; Rusk agreed. Critics said Rusk had fallen under Houston's magnetism, a charge which was unfounded.

Rusk's presence in camp was reassuring to the officers and men, morale improved and some reinforcements came in. "I find the army in fine spirits, ready and anxious to measure arms with the enemy," Rusk reported to President Burnet on April 6.[8]

Rusk and Houston agreed to move the army to the east side of the Brazos, a difficult operation as there were oxwagons and teams and some 200 horses to be transported, besides the "Twin Sisters" cannon which had just been brought in by Rusk's brother-in-law, Capt. Leander Smith.

The crossing was made on April 13 through use of the steam tug "Yellowstone," and the army moved on to Donoho's next day. There were murmurings in the army against Houston. Some believed he intended to fall back to Nacogdoches, in which case there was strong sentiment among the volunteers to elect a new commander.

Some 15 miles east of Donoho's the road forked, one route going to Nacogdoches, the other to Harrisburg where the enemy was arriving. As the army moved eastward, this was the point of crisis. Here again, there is disagreement among historians as to what happened. The brief biographical sketch of Rusk

8Rusk to Burnet, Apr. 6, 1836, Texas State Archives.

in the Texas Almanac of 1858, soon after Rusk's death, asserts that Rusk gave the order to Houston to take the road to Harrisburg.

According to this account, Houston called Col. Sidney Sherman to his tent while the army was encamped the night before reaching the fork and directed him to go through the camp and inform the officers and men that they would take the road to Harrisburg the next day—"that Col. Rusk, Secretary of War, had given him a positive order to move in that direction and that he was bound to obey the order as coming from his superior."

The "Texas Almanac" account continues:

> "Thus it will be perceived, the most decisive and the most memorable event in the history of Texas was brought about by the wise assumption of responsibility by Col. Rusk, at a time when the destinies of the Republic hung in dubious suspense. It is upon the pivot of his order that the whole weight of our subsequent history depends, and it was doubtless the realization of this, that induced the author Rusk to apply to Colonel (new General) Sherman several years afterwards, for a certificate of the facts as here related, which certificate was given, and is probably yet preserved among the papers of our lamented Senator."[9]

There was some minor confusion when the marching column reached the fork of the road. Would it be Nacogdoches or Harrisburg? The army took the road to Harrisburg — some authorities say of its own accord, without orders from Houston. A shout of joy went up from the men. "The turn toward Harrisburg was abrupt and enthusiastic," wrote R. W. Stayton. "It was the combined stroke of Houston, his officers, the President, his cabinet, Rusk and the army; but Rusk's presence on the Brazos was the direct and efficient cause."[10]

This event in Texas history and in the life of Rusk is of such critical importance that it seems proper to include the

[9]Texas Almanac of 1858, (Compendium, p. 62.) This unsigned article on Thomas J. Rusk has generally been attributed to David G. Burnet. However, Stuart McGregor, writing in The Southwestern Historical Quarterly, April, 1947, says the article was "probably written by Gen. Sidney Sherman." It was first published in the Galveston News in 1857 and later in the Almanac. Due to wide interest in the article, that issue of the Almanac sold 25,000 copies, compared to 10,000 for the issue before.
[10]Stayton, p. 12.

statement of Gen. Sidney Sherman, a gallant volunteer from Kentucky, who was among those urging more aggressive action on the part of Houston during the San Jacinto campaign. Years later, General Sherman wrote a letter to the editor of "The Galveston Weekly News", published in the issue of September 15, 1857, saying in part:

"Now I know this much to be true, that Gen. Houston did say to me at the time and place mentioned by you, that Col. Rusk, the Secretary-of-War, had given him positive orders to march in the morning for Harrisburg, and that he was bound to obey the order as coming from his superior, at the same time, directing me to so inform my regiment. This was about 10 or 11 o'clock at night.

"It is also true that Gen. Rusk wrote to me some time afterwards, requesting me to furnish him with a certificate of the fact, which I did. That Col. Wharton did as much or more than any other man to force Houston to fight on the 21st, I do not question, for his position as Adj. General, as well as his ability, gave him great influence which enabled him to accomplish much and I can assure you, sirs, that it required all the ability he was master of, as well as that of many others, to get the consent of the Commander-in-Chief to fight the enemy of that day."[11]

---

[11]Photo copy in Special Collections, Stephen F. Austin State University Library.

CHAPTER 9

Mirabeau Bonaparte Lamar to the Rescue

Jubilant though the army was at the turn to Harrisburg to challenge the enemy, the road was not easy. The route led through prairies, over land soft from recent rains. There were quagmires and quicksands to be crossed. In many places the mud was so deep that oxwagons carrying supplies and munitions had to be unloaded and the cargo carried on the backs of the men to firmer ground. The soldiers and officers put shoulders to wheels to help the oxen drag the wagons through hub-deep slush.

The spirit of the troops was much dampened before the haggard column reached the bayou opposite Harrisburg about noon April 18. There they remained until the next morning to rest from their wearying march and to gather information as to the enemy's latest movements.[1] The enemy had been there and, finding the temporary capital abandoned by the Texas Government and the populace, burned the town and moved on.

Both Rusk and Houston addressed the troops there on the 19th, assuring them that the time of battle was near. In stirring eloquence, the men were urged to avenge the death of their comrades at the Alamo and Goliad. Houston shouted, "Let your battle cry be 'Remember the Alamo!'" Rusk added that the cry should be "Remember the Alamo and LaBahia" (Goliad). Enthusiasm ran so high that Rusk stopped short in his speech, apparently feeling that the men need no further exhortation.

Rusk took time to write a rousing address to "The People of Texas: Let me make one more appeal to you to turn out and rally to the standard of your country . . . Santa Anna himself is just below us and within the sound of the drum. . . . We are parading our forces for the purpose of marching upon him . . . a few hours more will decide the fate of our army."

In his message, Rusk lamented the fact that "at the very

---

[1]Yoakum, II, p. 133.

moment when the fate of your wives, your children, your homes, your country, and all that is dear to free men are suspended in one battle," not more than a fourth of the men in Texas were in the army. "Are you Americans? Are you free men? If you are, prove your blood and birth by rallying at once to your country's standard. Your General Houston is at the head of a brave and chivalrous band, and throws himself, sword in hand into the breach to save his country . . . Rise up at once . . . what is life worth with the loss of liberty? May I never survive it!"[2]

In the same dispatch, General Houston added, "We are nerved for the contest and must conquer or perish. . . . We must now act or abandon all hope! Rally to the standard. . . . Be men, be free men, that your children may bless their fathers' names!

"Colonel Rusk is with me and I rejoice at it. The country will be the gainer, and myself the beneficiary."[3] The appeals brought results in recruits, though, of course, too late for the pending battle.

Houston also addressed a letter to Rusk as Secretary of War, justifying his action in giving battle at this time and place. He was taking precautions for the record in case of defeat or his own death. "We will use our best efforts to fight the enemy to such advantage as will insure victory," he wrote, "though the odds are greatly against us. I leave the results in the hands of an all-wise God . . . ." Apparently Houston was still reluctant and was joining battle against his own judgment.[4]

Leaving the sick and the baggage in charge of a guard detail, Houston and Rusk directed the crossing of the wide Buffalo Bayou to be on the side with the enemy. It was a most hazardous operation, made via a damaged, leaky ferry. Houston crossed with an early unit, leaving Rusk to come over with the last. It was the same process they had used successfully in crossing the Brazos the week before. When Rusk was safely over with the last group, the two leaders shook hands and Houston said, "Thank God, we are at last safely over!"[5]

[2]Houston's **Writings,** I, p. 415-16.
[3]Ibid., p. 416.
[4]Wisehart, M. K., **Sam Houston, American Giant** (Robert B. Luce, Inc., Washington, D. C., 1962) p. 221. Hereafter referred to as "Wisehart."
[5]**The Life of Sam Houston, The Only Authentic Memoir of Him Ever Published** (J. C. Derby, New York, 1855). pp. 112-13.

After the crossing, the Texans made a forced march along the Bayou, in the direction of the San Jacinto River, without a halt until around midnight. Then, after a short rest, they continued on to the San Jacinto where they arrived at Lynch's Ferry early in the morning of April 20. They camped in a grove of liveoaks at the edge of a prairie about two miles in width, with the river on their left and Buffalo Bayou to their rear. The Mexican force under Santa Anna arrived and took position on the southern edge of the same prairie, with marshes to their back. The forces were then about evenly matched, with around 800 men each.[6]

As the two armies faced each other that afternoon, the Mexicans opened fire with their one cannon, and the "Twin Sisters" blazed away in return, but neither side did any great damage. Colonel Sidney Sherman led a small group of volunteer horsemen in an attempt to capture the Mexican cannon.

In the skirmish which developed, a critical incident occurred which could very well have changed history. Colonel Rusk and Private Mirabeau Bonaparte Lamar were among the Texas horsemen. Faced by Mexican cavalry backed by cannon and infantry fire, the Texas unit was forced to retire, leaving behind Rusk, Lamar, Private Walter Lane and a few others. Lane's horse had fallen, Rusk was blocked by Mexican cavalrymen, and Lamar remained because he expected Houston to send support.

"As a lancer bore down upon Lane, Lamar swept over to save the life of his comrade; then he saw the Texan Secretary of War surrounded by mounted Mexicans. Digging his spurs into his mount, Lamar wheeled into the circle and knocked down one of the Mexican horses to make a gap through which Rusk escaped." Gambrell mentions that "an involuntary shout of admiration went up from the Mexicans at Lamar's exhibition of daring horsemanship, and the punctilious Lamar took a moment to acknowledge it with a bow before he returned with Rusk to the Texan camp."[7] Lamar bruised his leg in the maneuver and was noticed limping about camp next day.

The capture of Rusk, the Secretary of War, would have been a heavy blow to the Texas cause. He would doubtless have been held as a hostage, offsetting to at least some ex-

[6]Barker, The San Jacinto Campaign, p. 257.
[7]Gambrell, Anson Jones, pp. 68, 69.

tent the advantage gained by Texas in the capture of Santa Anna. Had he been killed, Texas would have been deprived of one of its greatest patriots.

As a consequence of the incident, Private Lamar was promoted next day to colonel and commanded the Texas cavalry in the Battle of San Jacinto—a step toward the presidency of the new Republic. Rusk may have remembered his debt to Lamar in later years when he stepped aside for Lamar to make a successful bid for the presidency.

CHAPTER 10

On the Field of San Jacinto

Thursday, April 21, dawned fair after days of rain and mud. It was a good omen. There was great expectation in the Texas camp on the San Jacinto River. Some doubt still prevailed among subordinates as to whether Houston was going to fight. Indeed there seemed to be some indecision on the part of the commander—or possibly he was only keeping his own counsel. Houston and Rusk rode out for observation about 10 o'clock that morning. There is no record of what passed between them. Earlier that morning enemy reinforcements had arrived. It was a force of about 400 men commanded by General Cos, brother-in-law of Santa Anna—the same Cos who had surrendered and been paroled at San Antonio the year before.

Meanwhile, Col. John A. Wharton, the Adjutant General, went about camp rousing the men to fighting spirit. "Over half of the men paraded, expecting orders, but, up to noon nothing could be decided." Some of the troops stood waiting in ranks for four hours. "Finally, Houston said to Wharton: 'Fight and be damned!' This was enough. Wharton again went among the men telling them . . . that it was now decided."[1]

Yielding to requests of the officers, Houston called a council of war with the field officers and Secretary Rusk. The question was whether to attack the enemy or wait for his attack. Some of the junior officers were for taking the fight to the enemy, but the four senior officers advised against attack, and Rusk concurred, saying: "To attack veteran troops with raw militia is a thing unheard of; to charge upon the enemy without bayonets, in an open prairie has never been known; our situation is strong; in it we can whip all Mexico."[2] This was good reasoning on the part of a leader with limited experience in military tactics, but Sam Houston ruled otherwise and, aided by fate, took the path to glory.

---

[1]Labadie, Dr. N. D., The Battle of San Jacinto (Published in Texas Almanac, 1859 Issue).
[2]Houston's Writings, VII, p. 319.

It was decided to attack at dawn the next day, but in this plan, the army overruled the commanders, voting to fight immediately.[3] With all the controversy and divided counsel, it is amazing that victory was ever achieved. Perhaps the very uncertainty and brashness of it all played into the hands of the Texans. Feeling that the "rabble" Texan army which he looked upon with contempt, would not be foolish enough to attack him in position, Santa Anna, as well as most of his officers, lay down for their usual afternoon siesta, and had not awakened when the attack came at mid-afternoon.

Thomas J. Rusk rode with the courageous Texans to the beat of the drum and the shrilling cry of the fife in the strange war music of a popular song of the day, "Will You Come to the Bower".[4] As the lines moved across the prairie, the suspense became almost unbearable as no fire came from the enemy. Were they marching into a death trap? There must almost have been a feeling of relief and a return to reality when a scattering volley of musketry came from the enemy lines, doing scarcely any damage.

The Texans had been ordered to hold their fire until they were in close range. The first deadly volley of the Texas infantry threw the enemy into confusion and rout. "Remember the Alamo!", shouted some; "Remember Goliad!", "Remember La Bahia!", screamed others as they followed up the volley, not taking time to reload, but using their rifles for clubs and their Bowie knives for daggers. Only a few had bayonets.

Colonel Rusk, who has written graphic accounts of other battles in the war, gave the first written report of the Battle of San Jacinto the next day after the fight. It is doubtless the most authentic record. He describes how Colonel Sherman's division on the left wing drove the enemy from the woods they occupied. "At the same moment, Col. Burleson's division, together with the regulars, charged upon and mounted the breastworks of the enemy, and drove them from their cannon, our artillery, the meanwhile, charging up and firing upon them with great effect. The cavalry under Col. Lamar, at the same time fell on them with great fury and great slaughter. . . .

"The enemy soon took to flight, officers and all, some on foot and some on horseback," Rusk's official report continues. "In ten minutes after the firing of the first gun, we were charg-

---

[3]Barker, **San Jacinto Campaign,** p. 258.
[4]Barker, **Texas History,** p. 302.

ing through the camp and driving them before us. They fled in confusion and dismay down the river, closely followed by our troops for four miles. Some of them took to the prairie, and were pursued by our cavalry; others were shot in attempting to swim the river; and in a short period the sanguinary conflict was terminated by the surrender of nearly all who were not slain. . . ."[5]

Rusk estimated the losses of the enemy at over 600 slain and above 600 prisoners, while the Texas losses were put at seven dead and 15 wounded. He reported that Major General Houston "acted with great gallantry, encouraging his men to the attack, and heroically, charging in front of the infantry, within a very few yards of the enemy, receiving . . . a wound in the leg."[6]

With usual modesty, Colonel Rusk did not mention his own name in the report, or refer to his part in the battle. However, he came in for warm praise in Houston's official report three days later: "Colonel T. J. Rusk, secretary of war, was on the field. For weeks his services had been highly beneficial to the army. In the battle, he was on the left wing, where Colonel Sherman's command first encountered and drove in the enemy; he bore himself gallantly, and continued his efforts and activity, remaining with the pursuers until resistance ceased."[7]

Though Colonel Rusk was stationed on the left wing at the start of the engagement, it had been prearranged that he should report to Houston after the battle was under way. Accordingly, he left Sherman's regiment and dashed across the battlefield, followed by his young aide, Dr. Junius William Mottley. Mottley was hit in the abdomen by a bullet and fell from his horse, mortally wounded. Rusk stopped to give aid, but was urged by Mottley not to delay his mission. Rusk continued and reported to Houston that the Second Regiment had made contact with the enemy in "gallant style."[8]

About this time, General Houston's horse was shot from under him. He was furnished another horse, which also went down with bullet wounds and the General wound up riding his third horse and with a bad wound in his own right ankle.

---

[5]Rusk Papers (Original) Report to President Burnet, April 22, 1836.
[6]Ibid.
[7]Houston's **Writings,** I, p. 420.
[8]Tolbert, Frank X., **The Day of San Jacinto** (McGraw-Hill Book Co., New York, 1959) p. 142. (Used by permission)

47

Rusk's 24-year-old aide, Dr. Mottley, died soon from his wound. It was said that Rusk loved him like a son.[9]

When the din of battle subsided, Colonel Rusk, checked on his younger brother, David, who was with a unit on the opposite side of the field. He learned from David's commander that the youth was safe and had acquitted himself well. At the close of the day, it was Colonel Rusk and David who lifted the wounded General Houston from his saddle, blood dripping from his boot.[10]

After the battle was decisively won, Rusk attempted to stop the useless slaughter of enemy soldiers. Some of the Mexicans were not without valor. A striking incident was related by Walter Lane: "As we charged into them, the general commanding the Tampico Battalion . . . tried to rally his men but could not. He drew himself up, faced us and cried out in Spanish. 'I've been in 40 battles and never showed my back. I'm too old to do it now.'

"Colonel Rusk hallooed to his men: 'Don't shoot him!' and Rusk knocked up some of the Texans' guns but others ran around and riddled the Mexican general with balls."[11]

Rusk experienced heights of elation in the sanguinary battle and the marvelous victory—emotion foreign to his true nature, such as citizen soldiers often feel in the heat of conflict. He exulted, not for his own feats, but for the cause of Texas freedom.

"This glorious achievement is attributed, not to superior force, but to the valor of our soldiers and the sanctity of our cause," he wrote in his report to President Burnet. . . . "This brave band achieved a victory as glorious as any on record in history. . . . It has saved the country from a yoke of bondage. . . . The sun was sinking in the horizon as the battle commenced; but at the close of the conflict, the sun of liberty and independence rose in Texas, never, it is hoped, to be obscurd by the clouds of despotism."[12]

Of the many controversies that raged in later years about the Battle of San Jacinto, probably the most bitter was over Houston's actions on the battlefield. Several witnesses declared Houston ordered the army to halt midway in the battle but

---

[9]Ibid
[10]Ibid. (Quoting Capt. Robert Calder) p. 162
[11]Tolbert, p. 146.
[12]Rusk Papers, Report to Burnet.

Colonel Rusk countermanded the order. Dr. N. D. Labadie, gives this account:

"I observed General Rusk, accompanied by Dr. Mott [Mottley], riding in full gallop on the rear and coming towards the left.

"On a sudden a halt is made in obedience to an order. Upon which Rusk shouts at the top of his voice: 'If we stop we are cut to pieces. Don't stop—go ahead—give them hell'."[13]

In General Sherman's letter to *The Galveston Weekly News,* quoted in part in an earlier chapter, he declared:

"Even this [the influence of Colonel Wharton] did not avail at the time Houston called a halt, for Rusk did, in violation of Houston's positive orders, take the responsibility of ordering the troops to advance—Although Wharton saw the great necessity for their advancing, and urged it as streneously as Rusk, still the Secretary of War, was the only person that could, with any propriety assume the command. On his doing so, Houston called upon men to bear witness that the responsibility would not fall upon him, and then he left the field. The battle was won, and the Commander-in-Chief has had no use for the witnesses he called upon."[14]

Houston denied to his death that he ever gave an order to halt. In later years he quoted a letter from Rusk in which the latter said the only order to halt which he recalled hearing from Houston was when some of the troops became entangled in a bog and he (Houston) ordered them to halt and reform their lines.

Houston and General Sherman had their differences, a matter which should be taken into consideration in attempting to arrive at the truth of the matter. Possibly Houston's words were misunderstood. At any rate, there was no rift between Houston and Rusk at the time, for each praised the valor of the other in their official reports of the battle.

From the mass of conflicting statements that have been written during the past 135 years concerning the Battle of San Jacinto, the author has arrived at two conclusions:

[13]Dr. Labadie.
[14]Sherman to **Galveston Weekly News**, Sept. 15, 1857.

First, Houston was reluctant to meet the enemy and, but for the prodding of Rusk and others, would not have fought at that time and place—there would have been no Battle of San Jacinto.

Second, that Thomas J. Rusk should share with Sam Houston the honor of the victory—an honor which, due to his inherent unselfishness, he never claimed and, up to this time, has never received.

At some later date, Rusk recalled some interesting incidents in the battle, not mentioned in his official report. One of these anecdotes told how he discovered Colonel Almonte among the prisoners.

"At the close of the fight and just before sundown," he related, "Colonel Almonte came out of the woods and surrendered with about two hundred and fifty men. There were at that place, not exceeding ten or fifteen Americans; and none of them could speak the Mexican language very well. The prisoners . . . were asked in the Spanish language if any of them could speak English. Almonte answered, in Spanish, that they could not."

The prisoners were given orders in broken Spanish to form in a column and were started toward camp. Captives and captors alike were weary and one of the prisoners dropped out of line. A soldier threatened in English, with an oath, to stab him with his bayonet if he did not get back in line. The Mexican officer quickly told the prisoner in Spanish what the soldier had said in English. Rusk overheard the exchange and came to a quick conclusion.

"You must be Colonel Almonte," Rusk said.

"You speak well," replied the Mexican officer in English.

Rusk then rode up to him and extended his hand, saying, "It affords me great pleasure to see you, Colonel."

"The pleasure is reciprocal," Almonte responded with his customary politeness.[15]

[15]Foote, Henry Stuart, Texas and Texans (Thomas, Cowperthwat & Co., Philadelphia, 1841) II, p. 309.

CHAPTER 11

Rusk Parleys With Santa Anna

"I am General Antonio Lopez de Santa Anna, President of Mexico, Commander-in-Chief of the Army of Operations," announced a strangely dressed little man, placing his hand on his breast. He wore the uniform of a private Mexican soldier but beneath his army jacket was visible a fine shirt with glistening studs in the bosom. "I place myself at the disposal of the brave General Houston."

Suffering from his battle wound, Houston lay on a blanket under a spreading liveoak tree. There was amazement and doubt on his face. It seemed incredible, but James A. Sylvester, the Texas soldier who brought in the captive was not surprised. He had heard other Mexican prisoners murmuring, "el Presidente," and noticed their saluting as he led his prisoner into camp.

Soon Secretary of War Rusk came up, along with Lorenzo de Zavala, Jr., the son of the Texas Vice-President. Both father and son had been engaged in the battle. "Santa Anna recognized young Zavala at once," Rusk later recalled, "and advanced to meet him with great apparent cordiality, uttering many expressions of kindness, such as are customary among Mexicans on such occasions; several of which I remember. Among other things he exclaimed, 'Oh my *friend*, my *friend*, the son of my *early* friend;' with which, and other exclamations in the same strain, he embraced young Zavala with . . . apparent feeling, and, I think, *dropping a tear.*

"Young Zavala returned his greeting with that deference which would have been due his former rank and power, but at the same time, emitting . . . an expression I have scarcely seen on any occasion besides. His look seemed to wither Santa Anna; and staring him full in the face, he replied . . . with great modesty, and something of a subdued tone, 'It *has* been so, Sir.' Santa Anna evinced plainly that he was much mortified."[1]

---
[1]Foote, II, p. 312.

General Houston and the Mexican President talked briefly through interpreters, Houston's limited Spanish being hardly adequate for diplomatic negotiations. After the early exchanges in which several different translators were used, Colonel Rusk called in Colonel Almonte, whom he had found among the prisoners the day before, and who now acted as interpreter for most of the two-hour parley. Rusk now did most of the talking for the Texas side.

During this conversation, Santa Anna "alluded to Colonel Fannin and his men," Rusk wrote in a letter to Lamar a year afterwards. "No one had asked him about the matter, up to the time he commenced the conversation himself. What was first said, I do not distinctly recollect; but as soon as he commenced talking on the subject, I gave strict attention to what he said.

"He did not pretend to deny the existence of the Treaty [under which Fannin and his men were to be treated as prisoners of war]; but denied that he had given a positive order to have them shot. He said the law of Mexico required that all who were taken with arms in their hands should be shot; that General Urrea was an officer of the government and could enter into no contract in violation of the Laws; and was going on with a course of reasoning to show the correctness of his position."

At this point, Rusk cut him short, telling the interpreter to say to General Santa Anna that Urrea had made a treaty to extend to Fannin and his men the customary treatment of prisoners-of-war, and that agreement alone induced them to surrender, "and that to shoot them in violation of that treaty afterwards, whatever might be the laws of Mexico, was *murder of the blackest character.*"

Rusk added the warning that if Santa Anna "regarded the preservation of his own life, it would perhaps be well for him to offer no palliation to a crime which would blacken the character of all the officers concerned in it and would attach disgrace to the Mexican Nation as long as its history should continue to be recorded."[2]

When Santa Anna said he wanted to end the war and would order General Filisola to retire to Mexico with the army, Rusk replied that Filisola would not obey the order. But the

---

2Ibid., II, pp. 253-54, Quoting Rusk to Lamar, Apr. 23, 1837.

Mexican General vowed that his officers and men would obey any order he issued.

"Then order them to surrender," said Rusk.

Upon which, Santa Anna rose in his dignity and proclaimed, "I am but a single Mexican, and you can do with me as you wish; but I will do nothing that would be disgraceful to me and my nation."[3]

Santa Anna by this time was quite exhausted and upset and requested a bit of opium, which was supplied. Eventually he agreed to issue orders to his armies to cease all combat activities, Generals Filisola and Gaona to retire to San Antonio and Urrea to Victoria until further orders under an armistice agreement between the Mexican President and Houston and Rusk.

However, Rusk did not believe the war was over. There was no assurance that the commanders of the thousands of Mexican troops still on Texas soil would obey the orders issued by a commander held in captivity. The Secretary of War issued a proclamation, calling for "one bold push" to complete the victory:

> "To the troops and People of the East: Express
> "War Department, Head Quarters, Army
> San Jacinto River, April 25, 1836
> "All troops on their march from the East, will report at Head Quarters as early as possible, marching by way of Harrisburg. For the present let all turn out, the enemy have been badly defeated, and are retreating precipitately, for the purpose of concentrating. One bold push now will drive them entirely out of the country, and secure Liberty, independence and peace to Texas. Let all turn out; our Standard is a victorious one and waves beautifully under the smiles of a beneficent Providence.
> (Signed) "Thomas J. Rusk, Secretary of War."[4]

As a matter of fact, it turned out that the Mexican armies were in no condition to fight, even if they had chosen to disregard Santa Anna's orders. Worn out by long marches, cut off by swollen streams, hampered by muddy roads, widespread illness and acute shortage of supplies, there was little choice but retreat.

Meanwhile, Colonel Rusk had dispatched messengers to President Burnet at Galveston, where the Government had fled

---

[3]Barker, **Texas History**, 303-4.
[4]Houston's **Writings**, I, p. 423.

bearing the report of the Battle of San Jacinto and a request that the President and his cabinet come at once to the army camp to discuss terms with Santa Anna. Pvt. Benjamin C. Franklin, a descendant of the noted Ben Franklin, and two other soldiers were assigned to carry the message. However, Capt. Robert Calder decided to accompany the couriers in order to see his girl friend in Galveston.

The messengers set out April 23 in a leaky rowboat. After many difficulties, battling wind and waves, sometimes towing the boat along the shore, the party covered the short distance to Galveston in five days and delivered the dispatches on April 28. President Burnet and the Cabinet members arrived at the army headquarters at San Jacinto aboard the *Yellowstone* May 4.[5]

Rusk and Houston already had drawn up a proposed treaty with Santa Anna. Burnet recalled later that among the first incidents after arrival of the Government party, and before any discussion was held, was the presentation to him of a protocol of a treaty, in pencil, "comprising seven or eight articles by Mr. Rusk, the Secretary of War." These, Burnet said, formed the basis of the treaty.[6] Bitter argument arose in the cabinet, some opposing any kind of treaty with Santa Anna, whom, they argued, deserved only to be shot.

Eventually, on May 8, two treaties were signed at Velasco, the latest seat of the Government—one a public treaty and one secret. In the public treaty, Santa Anna agreed never again to take up arms against Texas and to use his influence to end the war; all hostilities would cease and the Mexican troops, numbering 7,000, would withdraw from Texas; captured property would be restored; all Texas prisoners held by Mexico would be exchanged for an equal number of Mexican prisoners.

The secret treaty provided that Santa Anna should use his influence to secure recognition of Texas' independence by Mexico and establishment of the border at the Rio Grande. However, the secret agreement was never honored by either side. Santa Anna, with justification, claimed that it was abrogated by the fact that the Texans did not carry out their part by releasing him as agreed, and returning him to Vera Cruz. No part

[5]Tolbert, p. 203.

[6]Brown, John Henry, **History of Texas 1685 to 1892**, (L. E. Daniell. Pub., St. Louis, 1892) Vol. II, p. 53.

of either treaty was ever recognized by the Mexican government.

The bitterness of President Burnet and his cabinet against General Sam Houston flared openly before affairs at the battlefield were concluded. Houston was accused of mishandling the spoils seized from the Mexican army. Silver specie, valued at $12,000, which was captured was used by Houston to pay his soldiers who had gone for some time without pay. President Burnet and others of the cabinet said the money should have been turned over to the treasury as it was badly needed by the government. There was also talk about Colonel Almonte's fine stallion which the army had presented to Houston. The General gave the horse back. In a meeting of the Cabinet, one member proposed that Houston be dismissed from the service for misconduct in handling the spoils. Rusk, as Secretary of War, came to Houston's defense. He indignantly warned that it would be futile for the government to try to alienate the sympathy of the troops from their beloved General.

General Houston's battle wound was giving serious trouble and he was reluctantly granted leave by the cabinet to go to New Orleans for treatment. The ship, *Yellowstone,* was being readied to carry President Burnet and his Cabinet back to the seat of government. Surgeon General Ewing, who was caring for Houston's wound, considered his patient so serious now that he might die. Ewing asked permission for the General to be placed aboard the *Yellowstone* to hasten his trip to New Orleans.

Hatred had grown bitter indeed; the request was refused!

In the face of the furor, Thomas J. Rusk and his young brother, David, lifted the cot on which Houston lay suffering and carried him gently aboard. It was a poignant farewell of brave comrades. The government dared not remove the wounded hero.

The rancor that arose at this time continued to plague the affairs of Texas throughout the history of the Republic and early statehood. Houston was eternally slandered by his political enemies. On the other hand, never "thin skinned," he could take abuse and he could "dish it out." Scarcely a leading figure in the Republic, or later in the State, escaped his sarcastic words and his vitriolic pen. Not even his friend Rusk was always to be spared!

CHAPTER 12

Rusk in Command of the Army

Upon Houston's departure, Rusk was appointed to take command of the Army. He at first declined, writing President Burnet and the Cabinet that "it is a matter of great consolation to me that my conduct has so far received the Sanction of as enlightened a body as the Gentlemen composing the Executive Government of Texas as to merit this evidence of their confidence. I am from nature and from feelings averse to the holding of any office whatever, desiring to pass my time as a private citizen."[1]

However, "the whole army, together with President Burnet and his Cabinet, united in urging Rusk to assume the office."[2] He was also Houston's choice as his successor. It seemed to be the one point on which all in authority agreed. Rusk accepted the post of Commander-in-Chief as a patriotic duty and was advanced from the rank of Colonel to Brigadier General.

"I confide in his valor, his patriotism, and his wisdom," Houston said of Rusk in announcing his successor to the men of the army. "His conduct in the Battle of San Jacinto was sufficient to insure your confidence and your regard."[3]

General Rusk was immediately faced with problems arising from a violent dispute over the disposition to be made of General Santa Anna. President Burnet initiated plans to carry out the public treaty by placing the self-styled "Napoleon of the West" aboard the schooner, "Invincible," to sail for Vera Cruz. However, a great clamor arose from soldiers and others in Velasco and the frightened captive was removed forcibly from the ship by newly-arrived volunteers from the United States under T. Jefferson Green. A memorial from the army was addressed to President Burnet, insisting that Santa Anna be held until a new Texas administration was installed. Eventually, Capt. William H. Patton, with a detail of men, was placed in

---

[1] Rusk to Burnet and Cabinet, May 4, 1836, Rusk Papers.
[2] **Texas Almanac Compendium,** p. 62.
[3] Yoakum, II, p. 165.

charge of the prisoner and made responsible for his safety. There the matter stood for the time being.

The appeal for volunteers which Rusk and Houston had sent out on the eve of the San Jacinto battle was almost too successful. By the time the men arrived, the fighting was over and the undisciplined soldiers were a grave problem to General Rusk as well as to the civil government.

Rusk moved the army to Goliad to observe the movements of the Mexican armies and to see that they got out of Texas as agreed. The Mexicans were moving out promptly, but with the Texas army, there was the usual problem, shortage of supplies and equipment. On June 1, Rusk wrote to Lamar, who had succeeded him as Secretary of War:

"We are here in an old delapidated Town, with many unpleasant associations and have not one days provision."[4] In fact, he had been there several weeks without having received any supplies or communication of any kind from the government.

In the same letter, the Commanding General reported that 1,000 Mexican soldiers who had been stationed in San Antonio "are now passing in sight of our picket guards.—I have sent out to demand any property and Prisoners they may have in their possession, which should be delivered under the Articles of Agreement which if they do not do they will pay toll for the number of skeletons that now lie around us, or the number will be increased."[5]

Here at Goliad (also called La Bahia) Thomas J. Rusk delivered one of his most famous orations. At the request of citizens of the town, Rusk ordered a military funeral for the victims of the Goliad Massacre. The charred remains of the bodies, which had been partially burned by the Mexican soldiers, were carefully collected and placed in a single grave. Under Col. Sidney Sherman, a procession of soldiers marched to the music of a solemn dirge to the side of the mass grave. Rusk began his eulogy:

"Fellow Soldiers—In the order of Providence, we are this day called upon to pay the last sad offices of respect to the remains of this noble band, who battling for our sacred rights, have fallen by the hand of a ruthless tyrant. Their gallant and chivalrous conduct entitles them to the heartfelt gratitude of

4Lamar Papers, I, p. 395
5Ibid.

57

all Texians. Without any further interest in the country than that which all noble hearts feel, at the bare mention of the word *liberty* they rallied to our standard, voluntarily relinquishing the ease, peace & comfort of their homes, leaving behind them their mothers, sisters, wives and every thing they held most dear, they subjected themselves to fatigue & privations and nobly threw themselves between the people of Texas and the legions of Santa Anna."

Rusk here related how the patriots, outnumbered ten to one and cut off from food and water, surrendered under a solemn pledge that they would be treated as prisoners of war. After being held for a week and "treated with utmost inhumanity and barbarity," they were marched out under pretense of procuring provisions and "it was not until the firing of musketry and the shrieks of the dying" that they knew of their fate. Some attempted to escape, but were pursued by Mexican cavalry and cut down by the sword. The speaker mentioned that "a bare remnant of the noble band" now stood by the grave.

For the slain, he said, "it is due their mothers, sisters and wives who weep their untimely end, that we should mingle our tears with theirs. In that mass of bones and fragments of bones, many a mother might see her son; many a sister her brother and many a wife her once beloved and affectionate husband. . . . But we have a consolation to offer them; it is that their murderers sank in death on the plains of San Jacinto, under the apalling words, 'remember Labihia'." He continued:

"We can still offer them another consolation: Santa Anna, the mock hero, the black hearted murderer, is in our power; aye, and there he must remain, and tortured with the keen pains of corroding conscience, must oft remember Labihia."[6]

General Rusk reached such heights of emotion that he was unable to complete his address. He broke down in tears and even the hardened soldiers wept. In fact he stirred the grief and anger of his men to such a pitch that the commander was to have difficulty in keeping them under control. Rusk made no threat against the safety of Santa Anna or his followers now in Texas hands. After all, he himself had an important role in negotiating the treaty which President Burnet and the cabinet were trying to carry out, but the army was at the point of rebellion against those policies.

---

[6]**Ibid.**, I, p. 400.

In fact, a problem arose the next day after the Goliad address when General Andrade, leading the last detachment of Mexican soldiers from San Antonio, halted on the road to Goliad and sent a messenger to Rusk, asking permission to pass through the town. In view of the mood of the Texas soldiers, Rusk knew it would not be safe for the Mexicans to pass within their sight. He refused the request and Andrade was forced to make a wide detour over a trackless prairie.

More embarrassing was an affair in which the army held a secret meeting and decided to arrest President Burnet, seize the government and put Santa Anna on trial for his life. Lieut. Col. Henry Millard was delegated to go to the seat of government, now at Velasco, take Burnet in custody and bring him to the camp for trial as an enemy of the country. Millard took a few men and set out for Velasco, intending to keep his mission secret. Fortunately for Texas, one of the men got drunk in Quintana and boasted that they were on their way to arrest the President. At the same time, Colonel Millard met up with an officer of his regiment, Major Amasa Turner, and as a superior officer, ordered Turner "to proceed to Velasco and arrest . . . David G. Burnet; take . . . possession of the books and papers of his office; and . . . the books, papers and records of the Secretary of State, of war and of the Treasury. . . ."[7]

Major Turner considered the plan as bordering on treason and, instead of carrying out the order, notified President Burnet of the plot. Through the drunken soldier's talk, word got around of the abortive effort to set up what would have amounted to a military dictatorship and it reacted in Burnet's favor. The more settled people were disturbed at the prospect of a takeover by a disorderly army. Many of the men in the army were new-comer volunteers from the United States, bent on adventure, conquest and the spoils of war.

The whole plot was fantastic and probably never could have gotten off the ground. However, it caused General Rusk embarassment to the extent that he found it necessary to disavow any connection with the affair. "I state most positively that no officer ever was dispatched by me, or by the army under my command, either to arrest the President or in any way to interfere with the civil authorities of the country; on the contrary, a strict obedience to the civil authority has always been rend-

[7]Wortham, III, p. 343.

ered by me, as commander of the army, except in the extraordinary case of Gen'l Woll of the Mexican army, which I am ready at any time to justify." Thus Rusk wrote in a letter to someone who had inquired about the matter, his letter dated, Columbia, November 7.[8]

The Woll affair, refered to in Rusk's letter, had come about when General Filisola, ordered by Santa Anna to evacuate the Mexican army, sent General Adrian Woll to Texas army headquarters to confer with General Rusk on details of the withdrawal. Woll, a Swiss adherent of the Mexican cause, aroused the anger and suspicion of the Texas soldiers by his arrogant demeanor and by nosing about the camp. He was suspected of being a spy and feeling became so violent that he was arrested by Rusk's order for his own protection and sent to the civil government at Velasco for whatever disposition should seem advisable. President Burnet furnished Woll with an escort back to the Mexican army, but a furor was raised by the offended general who accused Rusk of illegally depriving him of his liberty and insulting his character.

"The principal cause of your being sent to Velasco was the preservation of your life," Rusk wrote in reply to Woll's complaint, "for let me assure you, such was the indignation of the people of Texas at your conduct, that you could not have passed with your life to the Mexican Army; and when ever you say that indignation was improper and unjustifiable, I pledge myself to prove . . . the contrary to you, and also to the world to whom you choose to my astonishment to appeal."[9] Rusk then recited the atrocities of which the Mexican army had been guilty in the war and concluded with an indictment of Woll for his spying activities in the Texan camp.

So far as Rusk was concerned, this letter of May 14 closed the matter, but President Burnet received a complaint from Santa Anna concerning the incident. Burnet wrote a conciliatory reply, saying the matter had been beyond his control and expressing his regret for the occurrence.

A cattle roundup, Texas style, provided some recreation and relief from boredom, while the army was stationed at Goliad. Wild and semi-wild herds of cattle with no ostensible owners, abandoned during the war, roamed the South Texas

[8]Columbia Telegraph and Register, Nov. 15, 1836.
[9]Lamar Papers, No. 363.

country. Under Rusk's orders, cattle pens were erected of cedar posts and rawhide. The first sweep captured 327 head which were driven to headquarters, helping to solve the rations problem.[10]

---

[10]Nance, Joseph Milton, **After San Jacinto.**

CHAPTER 13

Lamar, Rejected by Army, Blames Rusk

Sentries at the Texas army camp at Victoria challenged a Mexican on horseback. The rider asked to see General Rusk on an urgent mission. Carrying only his quirt, he was taken to the Commander's quarters. He told Rusk he brought a message from the Texas emissaries at Matamoras and produced a carefully folded paper which he had carried for days, cleverly concealed in the handle of his riding whip.

The message became known as the "Whip-Handle Dispatch." It was the Woll incident in reverse. Rusk had sent three officers, Major Miller, Captain Teal and Captain Kearns with four soldiers to Matamoras to receive from General Filisola some Texas prisoners of war who were to be released under the treaty. But when the detail arrived at the Mexican town, General Filisola had been dismissed by the Mexican government and replaced by General Urrea. The government had refused to recognize the agreement made by Santa Anna and had ordered Urrea to begin a new invasion of Texas.

The officers and soldiers sent by Rusk were arrested and imprisoned. Learning of the invasion plans, the Texans in desperation bribed a Mexican national for $200 to carry the message which Rusk now held in his hand. It told of the enemy's plan for attack, but heroically urged: "Don't delay a moment on our account. We are willing to be lost if Texas can be saved."[1]

Excitement raged in the army as preparations were made to meet the invasion. Doubtless it was welcome news to those who had been agitating for an invasion of Mexico. The development also increased antagonism against President Burnet and the captive, Santa Anna. It was at about this time that the plot was made to arrest the President, as previously related.

However, the fact that Santa Anna was alive and well in

---

[1] **Arkansas Advocate,** July 15, 1836, from clipping in Special Collections, SFA Library.

Texas hands served the cause of the civil Government. The captive general readily complied with a request that he write General Urrea to call off the invasion, doubtless fearing that it might cause his own execution.

Agitation in the army for trial and execution of Santa Anna, who was now held on Orozimbo Plantation, near Columbia, the new capital, continued. It abated only when Sam Houston, convalescing from his wound at San Augustine, took a hand. He addressed a letter to Rusk, explaining in detail the need for keeping the Mexican leader alive and stressing the disgrace that would befall Texas if he were executed.

Thus Houston appealed to the army through Rusk; the army respected his opinions and the agitation died down. In all the turmoil, Rusk had appealed to Houston to return and take charge of the disorderly army, but the General—though he still styled himself in his most recent letters as "Commander-in-Chief"—never returned to his command.

Thomas J. Rusk did not aspire to military honors—though he was often called upon to serve his country in the armed forces. He had not wanted the present command, but had accepted it as a patriotic duty—and on a temporary basis until Houston should recover and resume his post. At the time when every Mexican solider had retired beyond the Rio Grande and seemingly the emergency had passed, Rusk had asked to be relieved of the command in order that he might attend to his neglected affairs and be with his family from whom he had long been separated. He had recommended the appointment of a major general to take command but had made it clear that he would not accept the post for himself if offered. However, when information came of the proposed new invasion by Mexico, he apparently decided that his duty was with the army as long as General Houston delayed in resuming command.

Nevertheless, President Burnet and the Cabinet, possibly with urging from Lamar, decided to solve the Government's problems with the army by sending Colonel Lamar to replace Rusk as commander-in-chief. By the time Lamar arrived in camp, resolutions had been drawn up by some of the officers and men, without the knowledge of Rusk, opposing the appointment of Lamar. Some of the unit commanders said they would not serve under him.

For his part, Rusk recognized the authority of the civil

government. He received Lamar with courtesy, paraded the troops and presented the command to his successor. Lamar had been apprised of the opposition to him. Accordingly, he addressed the troops, dwelled upon his own record at San Jacinto, and declared that if his appointment as commander was not acceptable, he would "cheerfully go into their ranks and fight by their sides, and lead the van to victory."[2]

He called for a vote as to whether he should assume the post. "All those willing to accept him as commander were to march to the right; all others were to step to the left. Fifteen hundred men briskly stepped off to the left; 170 stepped to the right."[3]

After this shocking rebuff, Lamar remained in camp a few days, hoping for a change in attitude. On July 17, he wrote a letter to President Burnet, complaining of his treatment and blaming Rusk for his own fiasco:

"On my arrival, I was informed that I could not be recognized as Commander-in-Chief. I proposed to speak to the soldiers and did so, but was answered by Rusk, Green and Felix Houston [Huston] who carried the popular current against me. I had an open rupture with Genl. Rusk believing it to be the secret arrangements of his to supplant me. Some hostile correspondence; which instead of leading to further difficulties has resulted in this arrangement, viz, that he is to recognize my orders in the future. . . ." The letter continues with some complicated arrangements which were never carried out and a threat to court martial Green and Felix Huston if they "still maintain their present attitude of rebellion to my authority."

However, in a postscript to his letter, Lamar wrote that "Genl. Rusk says he will *now* stand by me in defense of the civil authority; he sees his own power departing as well as mine; the whole has been produced by his desire of promotion, and finding that his new allies are not aiming at his support but at their own aggrandisement, he is willing to co-operate with me; but I fear that nothng he can now do will be of any service in the

[2]Sterrett, Carrie Belle, **The Life of Thomas Jefferson Rusk** (Thesis for M. A. Degree, University of Texas, Austin, 1922) p. 66. Hereafter referred to as "Sterrett." Miss Sterrett did a thorough research of the sources available at the time of her writing and produced an excellent thesis, the most complete account of Rusk available up to 1971. She now lives in Austin with her husband, Mr. J. D. Harrell.
Also Yoakum, II, p. 186.
[3]Wisehart, p. 274.

cause of restoring that authority which his previous conduct has prostrated."[4]

Lamar was manifestly unfair in blaming Rusk for his own debacle and might be accused of duplicity in his letter to Burnet. Three days before the letter to the President, he had addressed a letter to Rusk, accusing him of blocking his appointment. Then, on the same day, July 14, he sent a follow-up message, saying: "From a conversation with our mutual friends Majr. Redd and Col. Smith, I am induced to believe that the letter I addressed to you this morning is the only obstacle to a friendly adjustment of our difficulties—As I am unwilling that anything to the attainment of so desirable end shall exist by my consent, I cheerfully withdraw that communication for the purpose of opening the door to a personal interview between us with the hope of restoring private friendship and public tranquility."[5]

Upon receiving Lamar's first letter, Rusk wrote a conciliatory reply, which was not dispatched when the letter of withdrawal arrived. True to his generous nature, Rusk did not harbor resentment. In the months and years to follow, Lamar was indebted to him for great favors.

Upon receiving notice of his replacement by Lamar, General Rusk wrote a confidential letter to President Burnet on July 4, 1836, saying, "I could have taken but one exception and that was the time at which it was made was calculated to have an unfavorable operation on me. . . . I have had but one single object since assuming the command and that has been to place the country in a state of defense. This the Cabinet have not done and of this I complained." He implied that some member of the cabinet, not Burnet, was trying to injure him.[6]

After a few days in camp, Colonel Lamar gave up the effort to win support and returned to Velasco, leaving General Rusk in command. There Rusk remained until Sam Houston was inaugurated as the first elected President of the Republic, October 22, 1836, and called Rusk to his cabinet as Secretary of War. His tour of duty as commander of the clamorous, unruly army had been a thankless job, with little honor and no glory. He had handled it as well as any one could, unless it

[4]Lamar Papers, I, pp. 417-18.
[5]Ibid., p. 415.
[6]Rusk Papers, Rusk to Burnet, July 4, 1836.

might have been Houston, who avoided returning to command in disregard of Rusk's pleas:

"First they mounted you & tried to destroy you, finding their efforts unavailing they . . . have been hammering at me and really trying to break up the army . . .", Rusk wrote to Houston at San Augustine on July 2. "A vast deal depends on you. You have the entire confidence of the army and the people."[7]

Strangely enough, Houston still languished in San Augustine "with his bandaged leg on a pillow, one of Phil Sublett's negroes in attendance and a Miss Barker reading from a novel. Miss Barker had journeyed from Nacogdoches to cheer the wounded hero. He said (but not to Miss Barker) that her blue eyes reminded him of Anna Rauget, who stayed at home."[8]

General Houston had opposed the much-talked-of expedition against Matamoras, Mexico, but apparently changed his attitude. Acknowledging a letter from Houston of August 9, Rusk wrote: "I am pleased that you approve the intended movement of the Army against the enemy and that you have concluded to use your influence to procure the cooperation of the vessels for the purpose of enabling us to effect. We are at War with Mexico . . . and one thing may be set down as certain, that the pride of Mexico must be humbled before we can expect peace. . . ."[9] At the same time, Rusk was writing Col. Felix Huston about plans being made for the expedition and the expectation that the cooperation of the Government and the navy in supplying boats would be forthcoming.[10]

In his letter to Sam Houston, Rusk pointed out that "we have now a larger army together than we can reasonably expect soon again to have . . . our enemy is now weak and distracted by Revolution without supplies and not entirely recovered from their late defeat and the question seems to me a plain one, whether we shall wait and see our army dissolved and theirs collect in heavy force . . or whether we shall begin while we are strong and they are weak."[11]

However, at about this time, President Burnet threw up the reins of government, Houston threw his hat in the ring

---

[7]**Raven,** Rusk to Houston, July 2, 1836.
[8]**Raven,** p. 264.
[9]Rusk Papers, Rusk to Houston, Aug. 9, 1836.
[10]**Ibid.,** Rusk to Felix Huston.
[11]**Ibid.,** Rusk to Houston, Aug. 11, 1836.

and was elected President. The new administration took over and Rusk was switched from Commander-in-Chief to Secretary of War. On September 22, Rusk wrote John A. Wharton that the planned attack on Matamoras had been abandoned.

Rusk had poured out his bitter feelings in his letter to his friend Houston a month earlier: "You speak of slander and abuse. My dear sir you have not felt its shafts compared with some others. While I have been sleeping upon the untented field pinched by hunger and worn down by fatigue reflecting upon the unprotected and suffering condition of my wife and three children, the pompous Lord of a hundred leagues of land who has never bared his bosom to the shafts of the enemy in defense of his lordly claims has been inventing known and malicious falsehoods to damn my reputation. I have been charged with being a military aspirant, a Tyrant who has subverted the civil authorities of the country."

The disconsolate General spoke of his efforts to keep the army together and complained, "all the return I have received was the improvement of every favorable opportunity . . . to lessen me in the estimation of every stranger who visited the seat of Government. These remarks do not apply to all of the cabinet. Some of them have acted differently. . . ."[12] Unfortunately Rusk's letter does not reveal the name of the enemy who was doing him harm.

---

[12]Ibid.

CHAPTER 14

Too Young for President

"I feel flattered that you should think me worthy of filling the Presidential Chair, but my age precludes me from running."[1]

Thus wrote Thomas J. Rusk to his friend, Sam Houston, in August, 1836. The war of the Revolution was over, the Interim President, David G. Burnet, had ordered an election in keeping with the provisions of the Constitution which had been adopted by the Council in March of that year. The two most popular men in Texas were now exchanging correspondence on the approaching election to be held September 1.

Rusk had been in Texas only 19 months, but during that time momentous events had occured in rapid succession. Texas had won freedom from Mexican tyranny and the "Foreigner Rusk" from Georgia had been involved in every phase. Even now he was only 32 years old, while the Constitutional requirement for the presidency was an age of 35.

With the mention of Rusk for the highest office in the new nation, something like a boom developed in the army, where Rusk was popular. Even the agitator, Thomas Jefferson Green, who had once renounced Rusk's military authority "pondered in his tent" and told Houston that Rusk would be "satisfactory."[2]

"I shall always feel under many obligations to you for your repeated evidences of friendship for me," Rusk had said in his letter to Houston declining to run. "This is an important office, not only so far as the credit of our Country is concerned abroad, but all important so far as our defense against our enemies is concerned. I would rather vote for you than any other man in the country, but we cannot spare you from the army."[3]

---

[1]Friend, Llerena, **Sam Houston, the Great Designer** (University of Texas Press, Austin, 1954) p. 74.
[2]**Raven,** p. 265.
[3]Friend, **Great Designer,** pp. 74-75.

Nevertheless, Houston continued aloof from the army command. He was nominated for President and Rusk for Vice-President at a mass meeting in San Augustine. Others joined in the boom and only a few days before the election Houston consented to run, saying "The crisis requires it or I would not have yielded."

Rusk, however, declined to be a candidate for the vice-presidency. From Army Headquarters at Victoria, August 31, 1836, a broadside was issued: "GEN. RUSK, highly sensible of the distinguished honor to which his friends are anxious to elevate him, by nominating him for the Vice-presidency of this Republic, and grateful for the confidence thus manifested, is nevertheless imperiously bound, both by duty and inclination, to withdraw from the canvas—duty, because the Constitution expressly provides for a particular age, (thirty-five), which he has not yet attained; inclination because he has not a single aspiration for office. With these views, and the firm determination to adhere to them, he most respectfully declines being a candidate."[4]

The official records show that Rusk was defeated for the Vice-Presidency by Mirabeau B. Lamar, though in fact, Rusk was not a candidate. Houston was elected President by a large majority over Stephen F. Austin and Henry Smith. Houston could afford to be generous. He appointed Austin as Secretary of State and Smith as Secretary of the Treasury. Rusk was named Secretary of War, the post he had filled so ably in the Ad Interim Government.

Besides the election of President and Vice-President, 14 Senators and 29 Representatives in Congress, three other matters were decided in the election: Adoption of the Constitution which had been written by the Convention in March; decision as to whether Congress should have the power to revise or amend the Constitution, and whether to seek annexation to the United States.

The Constitution over which Rusk had labored so tirelessly in March was adopted almost unanimously and the power of Congress to amend it was denied. Most of the 6,000 voters favored annexation, a goal which was ten years in accomplishment.

Though the Constitution of the Republic had been com-

---

[4]Lamar Papers, I, pp. 443-44.

posed in haste and confusion by a convention only a few jumps ahead of the Mexican army, it proved a workable charter and a credit to Rusk and his co-laborers who had burned the midnight oil. Its provisions were a combination of the federal and state constitutions in the United States. The executive and legislative departments were similar to those of the United States. Instead of division into states, the Republic was divided into counties. The Common Law was established as the rule in criminal cases and was to be followed to some extent in civil practice. Joint ownership of property between husband and wife, and forced heirship were departures from the usual laws in the American States. Otherwise, immigrants from the United States would find little difference from the laws to which they were accustomed.

As Secretary of War under President Houston, Rusk was saddled with the same frustrating problems that prevailed while he had served as Commander-in-Chief. The same rivalries among senior officers and the same insubordination continued. The swashbuckling Brig. Gen. Felix Huston had succeeded Rusk as commander. Felix and Sam pronounced their surname the same, though spelling it differently (Huston and Houston) and were remote kinsmen in that they were descended from the same Scottish and Scotch-Irish ancestry. But they never saw eye to eye. In fact, Felix was a thorn in Sam's flesh and gained command of the army through a strange magnetism which he exerted over the rank and file. The men called him, with great admiration, "Old Long Shanks."

President Houston sent Albert Sidney Johnston to succeed Felix Huston in command of the army. Huston, claiming that his commission of Brigadier General was issued prior to that of Johnston, challenged the latter to a duel. It was one of those senseless matters of "face" involved in the code duello. Huston had no personal enmity against Johnston but resented the action of the Government in replacing him. Johnston might have ordered his challenger arrested and court martialed as dueling was a violation of army regulations, but he would have lost the respect of the army.

"Five fires were exchanged without effect, Johnston not aiming," according to Marquis James. "On the sixth fire Johnston fell, seriously wounded. Huston rushed to his victim's side and acknowledged him the Commander of the Army."[5]

5Raven, p. 279.

70

However, Johnston was slow in recovering and Huston remained in command and soon forgot his promise to recognize Johnston's authority. Houston and Rusk issued a mild reprimand to Johnston but apparently did not give Huston even a rap on the wrist. The incorrigible Huston could get away with anything!

But if President Houston dared not cross the wiley Felix, he eventually out-foxed him. There was the ever recurring proposal for the Matamoras campaign with invasion of Mexico. This project was now being ardently promoted by Felix Huston and even General Rusk seemed intrigued by the idea. There was some conflict of opinions between the President and the Secretary of War. Finally, after Rusk had resigned, the President got rid of Huston by dissolving most of the army, leaving the commander without a command.

General Rusk resigned his cabinet post after serving only about two months. He gave as his reason the urgent need to attend to his personal affairs which had been neglected in the service of his country ever since he came to Texas. His reasons were valid. He had always responded to the call of his country when duty demanded it. Doubtless he now felt that with President Houston able and willing to handle the military affairs and inclined to do so, his services as Secretary of War were not essential to the public welfare. While there had been some differences of opinion between the two, the friendship was unbroken. Proof of this came when Stephen F. Austin, the distinguished Texas patriot, died December 27, 1836. His death made vacant the post of Secretary of State, which Houston offered to Rusk. The offer was declined for the same reasons that he had resigned his former cabinet post. At last Thomas J. Rusk was free to join his neglected family in Nacogdoches.

When General Rusk returned to civilian life, he presented his sword to John T. Murrell, a native of Mississippi—whereby hangs an interesting tale. Murrell later moved back to Mississippi and from there to California. But before leaving Mississippi, he deposited the saber in Belmont Masonic Lodge No. 90. A thief stole the sword and when one Anthony Foster found the relic, he was enraged and "in the heat of passion broke it over the thief's head."[6]

---

[6]Dallas Morning News, Aug. 15, 1942, Texas State Archives.

The story, as published in the Dallas Morning News, August 15, 1942, came to light when Ed Rusk of Nacogdoches, grandson of David Rusk, discovered an old letter written by Anthony Foster in 1859, offering to return the relic to some member of the Rusk family. The present whereabouts of the broken sword remains a mystery.

CHAPTER 15

Back to the Family Hearthstone

Having served his country constantly for two years, Thomas J. Rusk at last was permitted the comfort and love of the family fireside. From the dangers of battlefields and the privations of tentless army camps he could relax in the warmth of home with his wife and three growing boys.

The year 1836 had been a difficult one for Mary Rusk, filled with heartache, loneliness and physical dangers. It required all the courage and fortitude that she had inherited from her Carolina ancestors to meet the challenge of the new frontier. Added to the privations and horrors of a country at war were the dangers of savage Indian atrocities. It was a repetition of the struggle of the early American pioneers. Her grandfathers on both sides, Lieut. John Cleveland (called "Devil John") and Col. James Blair, served gallantly in the American Revolution. Her father, Gen. Benjamin Cleveland, was engaged in the Creek Indian War in 1813 and in the War of 1812. Her mother, Argin Blair, was a daughter of the veteran Col. James Blair.[1]

Mary F. (Polly) Cleveland Rusk was born August 14, 1809, being 26 at the time of her arrival in Texas. She was tall and slender, with dark hair and eyes which contrasted with her fair skin. Mrs. Rusk was described by associates as quite handsome, though unfortunately she had lost the sight of one eye, from some cause not recorded.[2] The evidence is that she was somewhat reserved in manner but was loved and admired by close associates and ready to extend kindness to anyone in sickness, sorrow or need.

Her letters to her husband reveal that she was poorly educated, which is not surprising in times when formal education was not considered essential for women. On the Texas frontier, lack of book-learning was scarcely a handicap.

[1]Jaynes, p. 33.
[2]Blount, pp. 190-91.

Mrs. Rusk had not been long in Texas when her courage was tested and proven. During the sweep of the Mexican armies across the country prior to the Battle of San Jacinto, the Indians in East Texas were restless and threatening. Mrs. Rusk with her three small boys joined the fleeing populace in the "Runaway Scrape." Hugh McLeod with a command of 30 men garrisoned the fort at Nacogdoches, provided the only protection for the fleeing families. Mrs. Rusk kept her poise and calmed others with the assurance, "As long as the brave McLeod or one of his men is living, we have nothing to fear."[3]

As the flight of the crowd proceed toward the United States border, the terror was increased by an occasional fleeing horseman overtaking and passing them. "On one occasion a dastard, of whom there were fortunately but few in Texas, took time in his flight to scream out 'Hurry up or the Indians will scalp you'."

"Mrs. Rusk, with undisturbed serenity, and with something of humor in her retort, replied to him: 'You will save *your* scalp if your horse holds out'."[4]

Mrs. Rusk remembered the protection provided by the "brave McLeod" when she nursed him during a serious illness some time later. McLeod wrote to General Lamar: "I have been but a few days out of a sick bed, to which I was confined nearly a month with the most violent fever I ever had. . . . Genl. Rusk had me carried to his house and his lady attended me with a mother's kindness—I feel under highest obligations to the family."[5]

General Rusk, who was with the armed forces at this critical period, was greatly concerned for the safety of his family. After he was made Commander-in-Chief, he wrote General E. P. Gaines, commander of the United States forces at Fort Jessup, asking for protection for his wife and children in case they were forced to abandon their home. Dated June 18, 1836, from Army Headquarters at Victoria, the letter stated that the Mexican forces were advancing 7,000 strong while Rusk had under his command at that time only 400, but was expecting reinforcements in a few days. The Mexican motto, he said "is extermination to the Sabine or death. Ours is liberty or death."[6]

[3]Brooks, Elizabeth, **Prominent Women of Texas** (The Werner Co., Akron, Ohio, 1896) p. 20.
[4]**Ibid.** p. 21.
[5]Lamar Papers, II, p. 197.
[6]Rusk Papers, Rusk to General Gaines, June 18, 1836.

Fortunately the Mexicans abandoned their invasion plans. In this period, however, General Gaines marched a force of American troops to Nacogdoches and they remained there some time as protection against the Indians who had been driven from the United States into Texas. These Indian tribes continued to be a source of danger during the era of the Republic and a source of controversy even in the Congress of the United States after Texas joined the Union.

Relieved of his public responsibilities for the time being, Rusk entered enthusiastically into the practice of law and the role of a common citizen in Nacogdoches. With his fame, personal popularity and keen legal mind, he soon built an extensive practice.

"Rusk was a grand man," wrote a contemporary, Francis R. Lubbock. "He not only had a great intellect, but he was amiable, kind and considerate. . . . history must give the verdict that Texas could not bestow too much honor on Rusk, equally distinguished as a citizen, as a soldier and as a statesman."[7] It was a just appraisal by a man of the times; nevertheless, Rusk has been much neglected by historians. Yet the lack of honor accorded him can be attributed to his own modesty and unselfishness which inhibited him from seeking the spotlight of public acclaim.

In his public life he was motivated by a compelling sense of duty, and his private life by a deep feeling of obligation and affection. During much of his life the two calls drew in opposite directions and he was torn by inner conflict. The fact that he was away from home much of the time threw upon his wife almost full responsibility for the rearing of the children. But Mary Rusk was loyal and loving and willing to sacrifice in order that her husband might be where he felt that duty required.

Toward his family, Rusk was deeply sentimental. While he was in the field with the army or elsewhere in the public service, he took time to write often to his wife, though few of his letters to her have been preserved. The most revealing letter available in its original form is the one written from Nacogdoches soon after his arrival there in 1835. The first part of this letter to "Dear Mary" in Georgia was quoted in the opening chapter. The latter part is so sentimental that to publish

---

[7]Lubbock, p. 82.

it seems almost an intrusion of privacy, but it is a part of the Rusk story:

"A line from her on whom I think so often would relieve many a dull day and Sleepless night. I often travel back in immagination to Scenes; often do I think of that day on which we exchanged mutual pledges of our love; often do I think of the little ones which indisollubly [sic] connect our feelings and our fate and I earnestly pray God that the time till we shall again meet each other, fond remembrance, will be but short. Then and not till then can I think of happiness and enjoyment. This world may have claims for others but to me it has none equal to the wife of my youth and my children. Imprint for me a kiss on their innocent cheeks and when you retire at night, when the beating rain and pittiless storm may possibly be raging over my head, talk to them of me and in return thro weal and woe, through health and sickness, pain or sorrow, I will think of them and you."[8]

The letter closes with a love poem of Rusk's own composition:

"When away from thee, my own loved one
And roving o'er life's shore
Fond memories of the past rush on
Of her whom I adore.
I think of hours neglected, fled
When choicest joys were mine,
I muse on moments long since Sped
With your true friends and mine,
I sigh for her whose halcyon Smile
Oft whiled away my ills,
Whose faultless, blameless loving guile
Still thro my bosom thrills
I dream of her around whose name
My fondest hopes suspend;
I sing of her whose faultless fame
The lips of all commend,
I sing of her whom as a *wife*,
A mother, sister, friend,
I prize far dearer than my life
And shall till time shall end—
My hopes my great ambition. pride,
With *Thee* are fondly twined

---

[8]Rusk Papers, original, Thos. J. to Mary Rusk, Feb. 15, 1835. Rusk's letters are entirely devoid of punctuation. Essential marks and capitalization have been added here.

76

Beneath thy smile and by thy Side
These hopes shall be resigned.
"May Heaven guide and protect you from harm and trouble And grant how soon we may in love's fond embrace forget the past absence.

"I am till Death your
"Affectionate
"Thomas J. Rusk
"Mrs. Mary Rusk, Clarksville, Georgia."[9]

Thomas J. and Mary Rusk were joined in Texas by several brothers and sisters from both sides of the family. Mrs. Rusk's sister, Ann, and husband, Capt. Leander Smith, came during the Revolution and settled in Nacogdoches. Following the death of Captain Smith, Ann married Jim Thorn of the same town. Three of Rusk's sisters with their families eventually settled in Nacogdoches: Easter, whose husband was Nolen L. Meroney; Mary, whose married name was Bruce, and Jane, with her husband, John L. Thrift. Two of the Rusk sisters, Nancy and Rachel, remained in the East.

Tom Rusk, the oldest member of the family, and David, the youngest, differing in age some 12 years, were bound by a relationship akin to father and son. David, in his teens, slipped away from the family home in South Carolina, to live with his brother in Clarksville, Georgia. Possibly he revolted at the firm discipline of his father, John Rusk. He remained in Tom's household until the time of his own marriage in Nacogdoches in 1843.

As a veteran of San Jacinto, David Rusk, at an age of barely 20, was named the first sheriff of Nacogdoches County and served throughout the ten rugged years of the Republic. These were days when a lawman had to be tough to survive. He was a powerful man physically, a decided asset for a Texas sheriff. A measure of his broad shoulders and wide arm-spread is evinced by a shirt, spun, woven and stitched by his wife, on display in the Old Stone Fort. His picture which hangs in the Court House at Nacogdoches reveals a handsome countenance. When Thomas J. Rusk was away on public service, he wrote regularly to David about personal and public affairs. These letters, preserved by David Rusk, compose a valuable historical collection.

Besides Ann Thorn, Mrs. Rusk had another sister, Cather-

---

[9]Ibid.

ine, and two brothers, John and James Cleveland, each of whom died at age 21, unmarried. James came to Texas in the summer of 1835 but it is not clear as to how long he remained.

Like almost all other planters in Texas, Thomas J. Rusk owned slaves and used them on his plantation and for house servants. Even before he moved his family to Texas he had some slaves sent from Georgia. Whether they belonged to him or to his father-in-law, General Benjamin Cleveland, is a matter for conjecture. At any rate, John Noblitt, who later became a Nacogdoches citizen, brought the slaves as far as Natchitoches, Louisiana, and there they refused to enter Texas without orders from someone in the Rusk or Cleveland families.

Noblitt wrote Rusk June 13, 1835, to come to Natchitoches himself or send James Cleveland—the negroes had been very cooperative up to that point and he hesitated to force them to go further. He mentioned that he last saw James Cleveland in Memphis and he was headed for Nacogdoches. Just how the problem was solved is not revealed.[10]

Negro slaves in the Rusk family were treated kindly and apparently loved their masters. Neighbors called them "Rusk's free niggers," so well were they treated. One of the men called "Uncle Wiley" could fiddle a lively hoedown. On one occasion Rusk brought Wiley a fine fiddle from Washington. "Uncle Wiley" played for most of the dances and balls given in Nacogdoches, being allowed to pick up extra money in this way. His wife, Eunice, was the house servant, and greatly loved by Mrs. Rusk and the children, who called her "Aunt Dinny."[11]

The Rusk slaves and those of the Clevelands back in Georgia were, in some instances at least, members of the same families. Letters between the Rusks and the Clevelands carried postscripts of messages between the slaves. "NB, the old negroes are all well and sends their love to their children," General and Mrs. Cleveland wrote in a letter to their daughters, Mary Rusk and Ann Thorn. "Peggy can git as good a dinner as ever and yet is our cook and confidential house woman. Tony calls the hoggs and Charley drives the wagon as trusty as usual. Quill is a fine boy. Rash & Mary are as well as usual, grunts sum."[12]

---

[10]Rusk Papers, John Noblitt to Rusk, June 13, 1835.
[11]Blount, p. 184.
[12]Rusk Papers, Gen. and Mrs. Cleveland to Mary Rusk and Ann Thorn, July 30, 1849.

Another letter from the parents to the daughters in Texas two years later mentions the slaves: "Say to Henry that his father, and mother is as well as could be Expected and sends their respects to all of their children. Will is a fine boy and has got a wife. . . . Charley is yet driving the wagon, makes more money than all the balance of us . . ."[13]

---

[13]Ibid., May 6, 1851.

CHAPTER 16

Rule of Law Comes to Texas Frontier

"We have battled against the damages and difficulties of the wilderness, the savage and of our common enemy. All this a savage might do. It is in vain we fight, it is in vain we conquer if we do not establish on this soil a Government of equal and just Laws that will protect the rights and redress the wrongs as well of the greatest as the humblest individual who claims the protection of our common Government." Thomas J. Rusk was addressing the first grand jury ever empanelled in Nacogdoches—possibly the first in Texas. His full, mellow voice, his lofty figure and his beaming countenance captured the attention of every one in the court room in the Old Stone Fort. He spoke with easy eloquence and simple style characteristic of his public speaking. Fitting the dignity of the occasion, he must have worn his black frock coat, vest, standing collar and silk cravat, giving him a striking and handsome appearance.

"I have seen the enemy sweeping on over our country in immense numbers carry death and destruction in their train," Rusk continued. "I have seen them met in their mad career by a handful of freemen and have seen the tide of war roll back to its source and the bloody tyrant go in chains, a humble suppliant for the poor privilege of living beyond the day of his Glory. That, Gentlemen of the Grand Jury, was a proud day, but the feelings I then had do not compare with those I now feel. I now see for the first time it has ever been done in this Country the imposing spectacle of discharging a Grand Jury in this house which has stood here upwards of one hundred years."[1]

The speech marked the close of the history-making September, 1837, term of the District Court. It was entered on the minutes, and the original is still preserved in the office of the District Clerk at Nacogdoches. The Grand Jury, in its report, had complimented the court officials and members of the bar

---

[1]From original minutes in District Clerk's office, Nacogdoches. (The reconstructed Old Stone Fort now stands on the campus of Stephen F. Austin University.)

on their services, and Rusk had been selected by the bar to respond.[2] In the same term of court, Rusk had served as attorney in the first court case tried in the Republic of Texas.

Rusk was not considered a great orator of silver tongue and flowery rhetoric, but when he spoke, people listened and usually acted in the direction he urged. When a cause was to be presented in the community, a few proper remarks to be made on a special occasion or an issue to be decided in legislative halls, Rusk was always in demand. Brevity and sincerity were traits that added to his popularity. As a trial lawyer, his mastery of the facts and law of the case involved, his logic and earnestness swayed juries and judges.

In Rusk's private relations, "he was hospitable and kind, beloved of all his neighbors." Democracy was a natural part of his life. "All were welcome at his house, the humblest visited him and were equally welcome and at home with the richest and greatest of the land," said Judge John Hemphill. In his family circle, "no word of unkindness to any member of his family was ever heard to flow from his lips. His wife, the partner of his bosom in youth and in age, in misfortune and in prosperity, was cherished by him with an indescribable fervor and depth of tenderness . . ."[3]

If Rusk had infirmities, "they were few in proportion to those which fall to the lot of man," declared Sam Houston.[4] Drinking to excess was Rusk's greatest weakness and he acknowledged this fault. Occasionally some contemporary mentions that Rusk was "on a spree." Yet by comparison with other leading men of the times, his intemperance was mild. He considered the use of "ardent spirits" an evil habit and warned his sons against it. "The habit of drinking is easily formed and almost impossible to break," he wrote—from experience.[5]

Thomas J. Rusk lived and worked in the midst of a robust, sometimes violent, society in the decade of the Texas Republic. Gun and knife fights were frequent, and ordinary fist fights common. More Texans probably were killed by each other during this period than had been slain by the Mexicans and Indians in all the wars. A party of men could hang a horse-thief and go scot-free. Murderers were tried, but, with the defense of

---

[2]**Ibid**
[3]Hemphill, pp. 32-33.
[4]Houston's Writings, VI, p. 465.
[5]Rusk Papers, Advice to Sons.

such able lawyers as Rusk, almost always set free by the juries. Gambling and drunkenness were the order of the day and betting on horseraces was a favorite sport. Crooked land-grabbers fleeced both whites and Indians.

Nacogdoches and San Augustine were among the more cultured communities but were beset by all the vices of the times, though possibly to a lesser degree. This part of Texas was occupied mostly by landowners with families. In hard times in this area, some of the grog shops might fold for lack of business. However, in towns such as Galveston, Houston and Corpus Christi, inhabited largely by bachelors, the saloons and gambling dens thrived.[6]

Dueling was one of the senseless, criminal practices in Texas of the early days. A Harris County grand jury in 1841 declared dueling, gambling and intemperance were "three of the most pernicious vices that ever befell the human family, the great springs from which all other vices flow." The most famous duel was that between Gen. Felix Huston and Gen. Albert Sidney Johnston, mentioned earlier. Gen. Sam Houston had fought one duel in Tennessee in which he wounded his opponent, to his own regret. After coming to Texas he was several times challenged but was able to laugh off the fling of the gauntlet. One such challenge came when he called ex-President Burnet a hog thief, but Houston shrugged off Burnet's challenge. Laws were passed against dueling but to little effect. There was at least one case in Nacogdoches County in which a man was fined five dollars for sending a challenge.

There was a touch of grim justice in the Wharton-Austin affair. At a political dinner, John A. Wharton, lawyer-editor, proposed a toast: "The Austins: May their bones burn in hell." The head of the Austin clan, Stephen F., was away at the time, but William T. Austin, a quiet and peaceable man, felt impelled to defend the honor of the wide-spread Austin clan. He was an inexpert shot and when his challenge was accepted, he engaged a neighbor to teach him marksmanship. So successful was the coaching that, by a quick draw, Austin disabled Wharton's right arm before the latter could fire.[7]

Even the educated and refined Dr. Ashbel Smith was forced into an "affair of honor." Though Rusk owned a pair of dueling

[6]Hogan, William Ranson, **The Texas Republic** (University of Oklahoma Press, Norman, 1946) p. 38.
[7]Gambrell, **Anson Jones, p. 44.**

82

pistols, they were never used and, so far as Texas was concerned, there is no record of his ever receiving or issuing a challenge. A puzzling letter has shown up in recent years, written by Senator John J. Crittenden of Kentucky, purportedly in response to a challenge from Senator Rusk. In view of the fact that Crittenden was usually a strong supporter of the Texas cause in the United States Senate, it is strange that any such dispute should have arisen. Anyway, the letter is in facetious vein, apparenly intended to smooth Rusk's ruffled feelings:

"Hon. T. J. Rusk
"Senate (United) States
"Jan'y 21st, 1847

"Sir—Your note of this day is re'd & the challenge accepted. Exercising my undoubted right to select the mode of battle, I appoint to meet you at Carmargo and fight across the Rio Grande with field Howitzers. As I do this entirely for your satisfaction, I shall require you to furnish the Howitzers with a suitable supply of powder and ball, and of provisions. The meeting to take place at some healthy season to be agreed on by our seconds and the notice of the time and place of the meeting to be given to the Army of Occupation and Generals Scott and Taylor invited to attend with all the force under their command.
"I have the honor to be
"Very respectfully Yrs & C
"J. J. Crittenden

"P.S. The seconds are to take part in all the hostilities to be waged.
J. J. C.
"Gun cotton not be used.
J. J. C."[8]

Tobacco chewing was one of the obnoxious habits of the time and prevailed among all classes of men. A visitor to the Texas Congress reported, "The way the members were chewing tobacco and squirting was sin to see." Francis C. Sheridan, an English diplomat, was shocked: "High & low, rich & poor, young & old, chew, chew, chew & spit, spit, spit, all the blessed day and most of the night."[9]

A church near Austin posted a sign in rhyme:

---

[8]Letter in possession of Forrest Sweet, Battle Creek, Mich. Published in **Texana,** Waco, Texas.
[9]Hogan, p. 38.

"Ye chewers of that noxious weed
Which grows on earth's most cursed sod
Be pleased to cleanse your filthy mouths
Outside the sacred House of God.

"Throw out your 'plug and cavendish',
Your 'Pig Tail', 'Twist' and 'Honey-dew',
And presume not to spit upon
The pulpit, aisles, or in the pew."[10]

Less objectionable was the sport of whittling, a pastime which Sam Houston carried with him to the United States Senate Chamber. Whittling, chewing, telling yarns and playing jokes on "greenies" were harmless pastimes. "Every Texas village had its 'loafers log,' where wits and tale-tellers had a ready audience." Knife-swapping was a natural side sport. If an argument arose, it was customary to say, "Put away your knife," meaning "fight fair." Such idlers came to be called the "Spit and Whittle Club."

President Lamar was called "the Father of Education" in Texas as he set aside land for a system of public schools. However, there was no market for the land and no public schools were established in Texas throughout the period of the Republic. A few private schools were opened.

San Augustine established a college, and Nacogdoches was not far behind. When Mr. Marcus A. Montrose came to San Augustine to take charge of the College, he was examined by the local committee. The questioning went something like this: "Can you figure? Can you calculate interest? Can you turn the grandmothers trick?"[11] (a card trick well-known to gamblers.) Apparently his answers were satisfactory. He got the job.

Thomas J. Rusk and Dr. James H. Starr started the movement for establishment of the Nacogdoches University. Funds were subscribed in cash, lands, lumber, labor and even pork. The Republic issued a charter in 1845 and supplemented the funds with a grant of four leagues of land. Rusk was among the liberal contributors. Mr. Montrose came over from San Augustine to take charge of the institution. The first term of school was held in the "Red House" in which Rusk and his family had lived at an earlier date. After 1852, other facilities were used

---

[10]Ibid.
[11]Ibid. p. 198.

Thomas Jefferson Rusk, from Picture in Old Stone Fort, Nacog-doches.

—Courtesy of Stephen F. Austin University

Mrs. Mary (Thos. J.) Rusk from likeness in Old Stone Fort, Rusk Room.

—Courtesy of Stephen F. Austin University

Rusk Memorial on Court House Lawn at Henderson, Texas
—Courtesy of Rusk County Chamber of Commerce.

The historic "Red House" which stood on the main plaza of Nacogdoches, first residence of the Rusk family in Texas.

—Courtesy of Stephen F. Austin University

"Santo Domingo Rancho," permanent home of Thomas J. Rusk family in Nacogdoches, long since demolished.

Monument at Grave of Thomas J. Rusk in Oak Grove Cemetery,
Nacogdoches. Small stone at left marks the grave of Mrs. Rusk.
Texas State Historical Marker at right.

David Rusk, brother of Thomas J., was first and only sheriff of Nacogdoches County during the days of the Republic of Texas.

Old Stone Fort where Thomas J. Rusk addressed the first grand jury, site of many historical events in early days in Texas. Reconstructed on campus of Stephen F. Austin University.

on a temporary basis from year to year until a permanent building was erected in 1859. This attractive building of red brick and Modified Grecian architecture still stands on the campus of the Nacogdoches Public Schools and is used as a museum.

The Masonic order was an important factor in the life of the Texas Republic. Rusk was a member of Milam Lodge of Nacogdoches and respresented it frequently in the Grand Lodge of the Republic of Texas which had been organized in 1837. Most of the prominent men of the times were Masons.

Anson Jones, then a congressman of the Republic, took the lead in organizing the Grand Lodge. The meeting was held in the Senate Chamber at Austin with "Brother Sam Houston" presiding. The Nacogdoches Lodge was represented by Congressmen Rusk and Douglass, Senator Burton, Charles S. Taylor and Adolphus Sterne. James H. Winchell "sat as a proxy for the brethren of McFarlane Lodge, San Augustine," but was expelled from his own Holland Lodge next day for "un-Masonic conduct."[12]

Protestant ministers were excluded from activities in Texas during the Mexican regime, as Catholicism was the only legal religion. When independence was achieved, missionaries came in from the states. Brush arbor revivals and camp meetings flourished. The fields were "ripe for harvest" and many converts were gathered in. However, the progress was comparatively slow. By 1845, not more than one-eighth of the white population were church members. Of these, one half were Methodists, followed in order by Baptists, Presbyterians, Catholics and Episcopalians.[13]

The Methodists with their system of circuit riders were most active and successful in gaining converts. They and the Presbyterians were the first to establish schools and colleges. Nacogdoches University was under Presbyterian jurisdiction. Rev. Littleton Fowler was one of the first and most famous Methodist missionaries. He established a church at San Augustine, said to be the first Protestant church west of the Sabine.

Rusk was invited over for the laying of the cornerstone with a Masonic ceremony, January 15, 1838. "Speeches were made by myself and Gen. T. J. Rusk in his clear and convincing style," Rev. Mr. Fowler noted in his diary. Three months later,

[12]Gambrell, **Anson Jones,** p. 118.
[13]Hogan, p. 198.

he wrote: "Happy am I to say that my friend and brother, General Rusk, is much reformed."[14] Rusk's writings reveal deep religious sentiments and firm belief in God, but it is not known whether he ever belonged to a church. At least he seems to have been much admired by Fowler, who had served as chaplain of the Texas Senate and there witnessed the trial of Rhoads Fisher, Secretary of the Texas Navy. "He [Fisher] stands impeached by President Houston," the minister wrote in his diary. Burnet and Rusk defended Fisher. Burnet spoke "with much bitterness towards the Chief Executive; his speech disclosed a burning hatred for the President. Rusk spoke in a manly style that was clear, forcible, and full of common sense."[15]

"The bachelor Republic was becoming tamer, what with Thomas J. Rusk and Sam Houston addressing Sunday-school meetings and some statesman getting married almost every month," Gambrell remarks. "J. Pickney Henderson brought to Austin the bride he had mirried in France and introduced Senator [Anson] Jones to her at church. . . ."[16]

Rusk accumulated a library of more than 1,000 volumes, the largest in East Texas. Included with literary works were his law books, public documents, volumes of "The Congressional Globe" and other works recording actions of the United States Congress. Many of the great historical writings of all times filled the shelves of his library room. Among his cultural activities, Rusk was one of the founders of the Philosophical Society of Texas.

[14]Fowler, Littleton, The Old Journal of, Texas State Historical Association Quarterly, Vol. II, p. 79.
[15]Ibid.
[16]Gambrell, Anson Jones, p. 192.

CHAPTER 17

Major General in Indian Wars

The Indians who, in earlier years, had been driven from the United States into Texas had, for the most part, remained peaceful during the Revolution as a result of negotiations by Rusk, Houston and others. However, as a part of Mexico's continuing harassment of the new Republic, emissaries were sent among the Indians and the Mexican residents to incite war against the Anglo settlers.

President Houston, having lived among the Indians and enjoyed their friendship, adopted his usual conciliatory attitude. He attempted to pacify the tribes and to restrain the Anglo land-grabbers who were encroaching on territory which the Indians claimed as theirs. His policy did not satisfy the angry settlers whose homes were being pillaged and their women and children sometimes kidnaped or killed.

Rusk was inclined to a firmer attitude and came to the conclusion that force was the only thing the Indians respected. Possibly the Indian matter influenced Rusk in standing for Representative from the Nacogdoches district in the second Congress of the Republic, an office to which he was readily elected. Depredations on the frontiers became so serious that President Houston called a special session of the Congress on September 25, 1837, in advance of the regular meeting date.

In this session of Congress and the regular session which followed came the first open break between Thomas J. Rusk and Sam Houston. It was the result of the fundamental difference of attitude on the Indian question by two strong-willed men. Rather strangely, considering the character of the two leaders, Rusk took the stern line toward the Red Men and Houston the side of charity, sympathy and diplomacy. Right or wrong, Rusk had the backing of the people and his policy eventually prevailed.

As chairman of the Military Affairs Committee in the House of Representatives of the Second Congress, Rusk was largely responsible for passage of a bill for organizing a militia for the protection of the frontiers. Apparently the Congress did not trust President Houston's policies and the bill was so worded as to take command of the militia out of the authority of the Chief Executive. It provided for election of the Adjutant General and the commanding officer by Congress rather than appointment by the President.

Houston vetoed the bill but, under Rusk's leadership, it was passed over the veto. Congress then proceeded to elect Rusk's personal friend, Hugh B. ("the Brave") McLeod as Adjutant General, Rusk as Major General, and four brigadier generals. Rusk's commission was signed by "Sam Houston, President", December 21, 1837.[1] Despite political differences, Houston had written to Anna Raguet on December 4, ". . . when I see such men as Rusk, and those who stand by their country, in the worst of times, my admiration is on tiptoe."[2]

Possibly the Indian problem could have been settled more humanely and with less rancor and blood-shed on both sides but for the activities of Rusk's old adversary of Revolutionary days, Vicente Filisola. The Mexican General, now in command of the military forces of Northern Mexico, with headquarters at Matamoras, carried on a campaign of inciting the Indians and Mexican residents against the Anglos.

These intrigues brought about what was called the "Cordova Rebellion" in the Nacogdoches area in the summer of 1838. Operating under advice of the Mexican commander at Matamoras, Vincente Cordova, a Nacogdoches resident of some financial means, incited a rebellion of Mexican nationals of that area against the Texas Government. A few Indians joined the uprising and a force which at times numbered 200 terrorized the people for nine months before being finally broken up.[3]

The campaign against Cordova and his followers began on August 7, 1838, when General Rusk learned that the insurgent Mexicans numbering more than 100 were camped on the Angelina River which flows east of Nacogdoches. On August 10, Rusk received information that 300 Indians had joined Cordova at his encampment on the west side of the stream.

---

[1]Copy in Special Collections, Stephen F. Austin State University Library.
[2]Houston's **Writings**, II, p. 163.
[3]Wortham, IV, pp. 53-54.

The General hastily assembled a force of volunteers. Strangely, President Houston ordered Rusk not to cross the Angelina.[4] Apparently he wished to avoid a clash.

However, Rusk disregarded what he considered a "peremptory order", and sent Major Henry W. Augustine and a detachment to follow Cordova's trail when he moved northward. The General himself led a force direct to the Cherokee main village, believing that to be the enemy's destination. However, Cordova moved rapidly out of the area in the direction of the upper Trinity, while the great body of his followers dispersed. Finding pursuit no longer practical, General Rusk returned to his headquarters at Nacogdoches and disbanded his volunteer troops.

"His Excellency President Houston has acted strangely," Rusk wrote to Vice-President Lamar. "Indeed had I been governed by his peremptory orders I have not had the least doubt that an Indian war would have been now raging here, but a timely demonstration of force by marching six hundred horsemen through their country excited strongly that which can only be depended upon in Indians, their fear."[5]

Adjutant General McLeod concurred in Rusk's opinion. "General Rusk's movements prevented, I have no doubt, a general Indian war," he wrote to Lamar.[6] However, the show of force did not long keep the peace. The Mexican-Indian bands renewed their depredations. General Rusk called out the militia of Nacogdoches County, some 230 men, and led them through the country of the Cherokees to the Kickapoo Indian village near the present town of Palestine in Anderson County. There the encamped militia were attacked by the enemy just after daybreak on October 15, 1838. McLeod related a dramatic incident, typical of the daring conduct which Rusk exhibited more than once in battle:

"The woods were very open and the trees large affording an admirable opportunity for their [the Indians'] favorite tactics of fighting behind a cover—and the morning was very misty, the commencement of a rain, which made it almost impossible for our men to see them; General Rusk with a view to draw them out, as he was entirely ignorant of their force, advanced about twenty paces and shouted—'You damned cow-

[4]Yoakum, II, p. 246.
[5]Lamar Papers, Rusk to Lamar, Aug. 24, 1838.
[6]Ibid., McLeod to Lamar, No. 846.

ardly————————, come out and show yourselves like men.' They made no reply except the yell and their rifles. . . ."[7]

After a few minutes of fighting, Rusk ordered a charge and the enemy fled, leaving 11 dead on the battlefield and suffering a total loss estimated at 30 killed. Eleven of the Texas militiamen were wounded but none killed.

The Texas House of Representatives commended Rusk's policies and expressed full confidence in him in a resolution which was adopted unanimously November 10:

> "Resolved by the House of Representatives of the Republic of Texas, That the Conduct of Genl. Thos. J. Rusk in the Campaign against the Mexicans and Indians so far as it has come to their knowledge, meets their full and entire approbation, And that they feel the fullest confidence in the gallantry, patriotism, devotion, and ability of the said Genl. Rusk to carry out the Campaign to a Successful termination."[8]

However, a few days later, retiring President Sam Houston, in his farewell address to Congress, criticized that body for limiting his power by placing the authority and money in the hands of the Major General and condemned Rusk for "encroaching upon the power of the President" in his campaign during the Cordova Rebellion.[9]

Soon the Indians and their Mexican agitators were again on the rampage and Rusk once more took up the sword. He was resentful of President Houston's criticism and expressed his hurt feelings in a letter to David Rusk from army Headquarters at Fort Houston (near present Palestine):

> "I am just taking up the line of march . . . to the place where the Indians are said to be encamped which is about twenty-five miles from here. Their numbers are variously estimated at from one hundred and fifty to six hundred warriors. My effective force will be under two hundred men—I know well that should I succeed no one will find fault but should I fail I shall be abused for imprudence. If Gen. Houston and some others had been guided by feelings of Patriotism and not by low and selfish purposes, I should have had in the field at least five hundred men, but let success or misfortune attend my efforts, I have

---

[7]**Ibid.**
[8]Rusk Papers.
[9]Journals of the House of Representatives, Third Congress, 1838, pp. 87-94.

the consolation of knowing that all my efforts have been devoted to my Countrys good. If the Indians are not routed the frontier will be laid in ruins. . . ."

There was a touch of pathos and a note of foreboding at the end of the letter. As often before and afterwards, he was confiding to David feeling which he could reveal to no one else: "Towards the people of Texas, I have no unkind feelings. They have more than remunerated me by their good feelings for all the sacrifices I have made and the services I have rendered them." As to a few "demagogues and speculators who, while I was doing all I could for the Country, were slandering me and speculating on the resources of the Country, I wish no greater harm than that they be changed into honest men."

He closed his letter with a despondent reflection: "If cut off, I shall leave my wife and children much less than many men have sold lots for in the City of Houston who never paid anything for them except a sacrifice of principle."[10]

---

[10]Rusk Papers, Thos. J. to David Rusk, Oct. 14, 1838; also Blount, p. 280.

CHAPTER 18

A Man Without Fear

One of Rusk's Indian campaigns brought about an international diplomatic incident between the Republic of Texas and the United States when the doughty Texas General chased a band of Caddoes across the boundary line into Louisiana. A tempest flared in the Louisiana press and the Governor of Louisiana lodged a protest against the "armed invasion" of American territory.

The Caddoes had been expelled from the United States in 1835 and were now living on the Texas side of the Louisiana border—a line which had never been clearly defined. Like other tribes, they were being incited by Mexican agents to ravages against white residents. Protests were made to the United States about the forcing of these and other Indians into Texas but with no satisfactory results. Rusk wrote Vice President Lamar that "you would do the country great service in my opinion by demanding of the U. S. a removal of all the U. S. Indians agreeably to the Treaty between Mexico and the U. S."[1] The treaty referred to was made in 1831, before Texas declared independence.

A new bill, hurriedly passed by the Third Congress and signed by President Houston November 6, 1838, appropriated $20,000 to equip 250 men "to quell the insurrection now existing among Indians and Mexicans."[2] Under this act, Rusk proceeded to Red River and Fannin Counties and enlisted militia. With a force of 70 men, he marched to the camp of the Caddoes near Port Caddo on the Louisiana border.

"Just before reaching their camp several guns were fired at our spies without effect," Rusk related in his report to the Secretary of War, and continued:

> "I dismounted the men and was about giving orders to charge when the Interpreter who was a little in advance, told me that the Indians said they did not wish to fight

[1]Lamar Papers, Rusk to Lamar Nov. 17, 1838.
[2]Gammel, H. P. N., **Laws of Texas** (Austin, 1898), II, p. 3.

but desired to hold a talk. I requested the Interpreter to tell their principal men to meet me halfway between the lines and we would hold a talk. I took Col. McLeod and met their head men as proposed. I told them they must surrender their arms to be deposited at Shreve Port subject to their order as soon as the war was terminated, and in the meantime not cross the Texian line. The chief said his only means of securing a support was with his arms, and if he surrendered them his people would starve."[3]

In this instance, Rusk proved that he was not without compassion for the plight of the Indians who were being buffeted between the two countries. He told the Indian Chief that Texas would support his people until an arrangement could be worked out with the United States. The Indians accepted these terms and Rusk and McLeod marched them to Shreveport where the arms were deposited with the U. S. Indian agent, Charles A. Sewell.[4]

It was for this action that General Rusk was bitterly attacked in the American press and citicized by the Governor of Louisiana. There was even a stir in the United States House of Representatives. However, the "Red River Patriot" of Shreveport, La., came to his defense in a warm editorial:

"We are sorry to see the periodicals of the country, commenting so severely on this celebrated General's 'late invasion of our Territory'. We admit that the General's march into Caddo Parish was to all appearances, an infringement of the law of nations—but we should remember the motive by which he seemed to be actuated. He believed that a band of Indians, after committing depredations on the Texians had entered the United States Territory with the intention of remaining here, so long as the pursuit . . . of them continued, and then, in accordance with their murdering propensities, to repeat aggressions. He came, and was his conduct when here marked by any contempt for authorities? No! The agent himself states to the contrary. —After threatening the Indians, if they repeated hostilities, he peacably returned.

". . . let us remember that he has shown himself a brave soldier—a firm patriot and philanthropic liberalist

---

[3]Rusk to Secretary of War, Dec. 1, 1838, "Indian Affairs" Papers, Texas State Library.
[4]**Ibid.**

—who periled his fortune and his blood in the cause of an oppressed country—at present arrayed in support of the glorious principles of our own Revolution."[5]

* * * *

It was a tense moment on a hot July day for the big brass of the Texas Republic—General Rusk, Acting-President Burnet, Secretary-of-War Johnston, Adjutant General McLeod and others—in the midst of an enemy Indian Camp, surrounded by angry, threatening Cherokee warriors.

The Texan army and Chief Bowles' tribesmen had been lined up for battle several days while negotiations went on between the leaders of the two sides. A neutral line had been set up between the two camps with an agreement that no one on either side was to cross the line without notice. But while the Texas negotiators were parleying with chiefs in the Indian camp, young John Bowles, son of the head chief, and a few followers crossed the neutral line. They were chased by Texas soldiers and when they reached camp reported that they had been run in by the Texans. This caused great excitement and anger among the Indians and it seemed for a time that they were about to attack and probably massacre the Texas officials who had entered the camp on a truce. However, explanations were made and order restored, but on future visits the Texas officials took with them an escort of thirty picked men.[6]

The incident occurred in July, 1839, during the administration of President Mirabeau B. Lamar. When he succeeded Houston as President, Lamar immediately adopted a stern policy toward the Indians and their Mexican agitators. By that time, most of the tribes had been driven from East Texas except the Cherokees, the largest, most civilized, and in the past, the most friendly of all the Texas Indians. However, in view of the troubles which had been caused by Indians and Mexicans since 1836, together with reports that Mexican officials were now conspiring with the Cherokees for all out war against the whites, Lamar adopted a stern policy. He resolved to move the Cherokees from East Texas, by peaceful means if possible, or by force if necessary. He proposed to

[5]**Red River Patriot**, Shreveport, La., March 15, 1839, Quoted by Blount pp. 282-83.
[6]Reagan, John H., **Expulsion of the Cherokees from East Texas**, Article in **Texas Historical Association Quarterly** (Austin), I, pp. 42-43.

pay the Cherokees for their fixed improvements, but not for the land they occupied as he considered they had no claim on the land.[7]

To carry out this policy, he appointed a high-ranking commission, composed of Vice-President David G. Burnet, Secretary-of-War Albert Sidney Johnston, Adjutant General Hugh McLeod and Major General Thomas J. Rusk. The commission proceeded to the Indian country and opened negotiations, and Lamar ordered the assembly of a force of Texas regulars, volunteers and militia to back them up in case peaceful means failed.[8]

After three days of negotiation, terms were agreed upon under which the Indians were to leave the country and receive payment for their improvements. It was in the course of these negotiations that the Texas leaders were caught in the crisis in the Indian camp. The Indians never signed the treaty. It developed that War Chief Bowles had been buying time for the arrival of reinforcements. The Texans also were expecting reinforcements and the battle was briefly delayed. The first engagement took place July 15, 1839, on the Neches River, near the Cherokee Village. General Rusk was in immediate command of the Nacogdoches Regiment, Colonel Burleson and Colonel Landrum headed other units and Brig. Gen. Kelsey H. Douglass was the over-all commander. It was Rusk's unit which made first contact with the enemy. "The enemy displayed their forces on the point of a hill . . . General Rusk motioned to them to come on . . ."[9]

It was a favorite military tactic of Rusk to draw the enemy out. This time the enemy came out and a sharp battle resulted. The Cherokees fled when a charge was made, leaving 18 dead. The Texans lost three killed and five wounded. The main battle was fought next day, July 16, when the Texans attacked the Indians in a new position. The bloody battle lasted an hour and a half and the Indians were completely routed. The Texans lost five killed and 27 wounded. Among the wounded in the two days' battles were Vice-President Burnet, General Johnston, Adjutant General McLeod and David Rusk, none dangerously. General Rusk was unhurt.[10]

---

[7]Brown, **History of Texas**, II, pp. 161-62.
[8]**Ibid.**, p. 162.
[9]Yoakum, II, p. 268.
[10]Brown, II, p. 163.

Losses of the Indians were estimated at 100 killed and wounded. Among the dead was heroic Chief Bowles who had led his warriors with great valor. Bereft of their leader, the Cherokees migrated to the area west of Arkansas or scattered elsewhere. East Texas was freed of all Indian tribes. The lands they had occupied were surveyed into sections and sold under an act of Congress in 1840.[11]

Expulsion of the Cherokees from Texas and the death of Chief Bowles brought a bitter outburst from Sam Houston. Striking out at Lamar's harsh Indian policy in a speech at Nacogdoches he shouted that The Bowl was a better man than his "murderers". There were angry threats as he left the hall. There was little sympathy for the Indians in the Redlands. Even such old friends as Henry Raguet, Adolphus Sterne and Thomas J. Rusk were offended.

Rusk was convinced that expulsion of the Indians from East Texas was inevitable. It was the process over and over as the American frontier moved from the Atlantic seaboard westward. "Yet let it not be understood that all of the right was with the whites and all the wrong with the Indians," observed J. H. Brown in his "History of Texas." "From their stand-point, the Cherokees believed that they had a moral, equitable, and at least, a quasi-legal right to the country, and such in truth they had. But between Mexican emissaries on the one hand, and mischievous Indians on the other, and the grasping desire of unprincipled land-grabbers . . . one wrong produced a counter wrong until blood flowed and women and children were sacrificed by the more lawless of the Indians. . . . All the Indians were not bad, nor were all the whites good."[12]

With the conclusion of the Cherokee campaign, Rusk's war days were over. He had led troops in half a dozen engagements for the liberation and defense of his country and never lost a battle. By contrast, Sam Houston fought only one battle in Texas and won international fame. Binkley remarks that "Houston could frame idealistic proclamations and appeals and then engage in petty bickerings which destroyed his usefulness to the army, only to become the military hero

---

[11]Gammel, II, 358.
[12]Brown, II, 164.

of Texas through a single victory which may or may not have been accidental."[13]

In war, Rusk was a man without fear and seemingly possessed a charmed life. It will be recalled that at the siege of Bexar, he led his troops to the shadow of the enemy walls to entice them to combat. In the Grass Fight, he charged fearlessly to the relief of threatened comrades. In the skirmish on the eve of San Jacinto, he had a narrow escape, then went charging about every part of the battlefield in the main conflict next day. In the battle with the Mexican and the Indian raiders near Kickapoo village, he advanced in front of the line and cursed the hidden enemy to come out and fight. Again at the Neches, he taunted the Indians to come on to battle.

Among other prominent patriots, several suffered wounds. At San Jacinto, Rusk's aide fell mortally wounded and General Houston was badly hurt. In the battle with the Cherokees, Burnet, Johnston, McLeod and David Rusk all received wounds. But Rusk, impervious to danger, went through his entire war career without a wound.

Daring in war, Rusk also was courageous in his stand on issues affecting the welfare of his country. He was loyal to friends such as Houston, Lamar and Calhoun and generous in making sacrifices in their behalf where his personal affairs were involved. But when differences of opinion arose concerning public policies, he had the courage to stand for his convictions as to what was best for Texas and its people regardless of personal friendships.

---

[13]Binkley in Introduction to **Official Correspondence of the Texan Revolution.**

CHAPTER 19

Mister Chief Justice

During the period of the Indian Wars, a presidential election had been held. Even in the fall of 1837, when Thomas J. Rusk was serving in the House of Representatives of the Second Congress, political activities began, looking toward the election of 1838 when Houston's two-year term would expire. Under the constitution, the first President of the Republic served two years and was ineligible for re-election, and thereafter the presidential term was set at three years with the incumbent ineligible for re-election.

There were no political parties but the campaign developed along the lines of pro-Houston and anti-Houston. Vice-President Lamar was ambitious for the office of President and was boomed by his friends as early as May, 1837. Houston supporters wanted Rusk, who, in spite of some differences with the President, was still regarded as Houston's friend and was favored by Houston himself. Francis R. Lubbock, youthful new-comer and Houston protege, led a campaign to nominate Rusk. Groups throughout the Republic held rallies and urged Rusk to run.[1] The election was to be held September 3 and the new presidential term would begin the second Monday in December, 1838.

"Rusk was the only man in Texas who could show the shadow of a claim as the peer of Gen. Houston in the esteem, admiration and love of the people," wrote John S. Ford.

"He was simple in his manners, republican in his tastes, candid and outspoken in the expression of his sentiments, fair and honest in everything. He had a giant intellect, mastered questions as if by intuition and was great without ambition and pride."[2]

With an eye on Rusk's wide popularity, Lamar hesitated in

---

[1]Lubbock, p. 82; Yoakum, II pp. 244-45.
[2]Ford, John Salmon, **Rip Ford's Texas**, ed. by Oats, Stephen B. (University of Texas Press, Austin, 1963) pp. 17-18.

making an announcement. Rusk was in position to carry the Houston faction and at the same time receive the support of a large segment of those who were disgruntled with Houston—particularly those who were bitter over the President's soft Indian policy and his failure to act vigorously against Mexico's harassment. Rusk had dealt effectively with the Indians and favored reprisals against Mexico. To these assets must be added his popularity with the army, which had rejected Lamar in 1836.

Nominally, at least, Rusk and Lamar were friends and Lamar solved his dilemma by addressing a friendly letter to General Rusk on December 7, 1837:

"I have received a letter from several distinguished gentlemen, our mutual friends, inviting me to become a candidate for the next Presidency. As you have been spoken of very extensively for the same high office, I am anxious to see you before I give a final answer. . . . I shall be in my room at 2 o'clock, when I hope it will be convenient for you to call upon me."[3]

Rusk did not find it "convenient" to call at 2 o'clock but wrote Lamar: "I hope you will not on my account, have a hesitancy in giving your consent to the request alluded to, as there is no desire on my part to have my name before the people for any office whatever." He added that "I feel bound to discharge to the best of my abilities, the duties of my station [member of the House of Representatives]; but beyond this, my private affairs and domestic obligations so long neglected, imperiously demand my attention, and will not permit me to think of public life beyond the discharge of those military obligations in the hour of danger, which I hold paramount to all other considerations." The mention of military obligations apparently refered to his new election as Major General of the Militia and approaching Indian wars.

While the letter did not commit Rusk to the actual support of Lamar, it did say: "But I shall be pleased, dear sir, to see your name before the people for the office of Chief Magistrate, and shall be happy to sustain you in your labors for the welfare of our country, to which we are both under many obligations for confidence reposed and honors conferred."[4]

---

[3]Lamar Papers, I, p. 591.
[4]Ibid.

As time for the election drew nearer, friends of Rusk grew more and more insistent that he make the race. Resolutions favoring him for President were adopted at a meeting in Houston May 15, 1838, and a committee representing all areas of the Republic was appointed to call upon him. Rusk was flattered and deeply moved; but continued firm in his decision not to run for the Presidency. In a lengthy reply to the committee, he mentioned his earlier statement to Lamar that he would not enter the race.

"I feel . . . the strongest obligations to our country, and am, as I have ever been ready to risk, or if necessary sacrifice my life in her behalf . . . I am, however, gentlemen, poor and involved in pecuniary embarrassments. I have . . . a large family solely dependent on my exertions for a support—not only my own, but another family, the charge of which by the death of a brother-in-law . . . has devolved upon me."[5] The brother-in-law referred to was Capt. Leander Smith, a veteran of San Jacinto.

In declining the nomination, General Rusk also mentioned the matter of his age. He would not be 35 at the time of the election but would be on December 5, prior to inauguration, a matter which might be "subject to different constructions."[6]

Rusk's refusal of the nomination was read at a meeting in Houston two days later and the assemblage voted support for Lamar. With Rusk out of the running, the Houston faction nominated Peter W. Grayson. After accepting the nomination, Grayson made a visit to Kentucky and enroute home, shot himself, reportedly over a love affair. The Houston forces then nominated James Collingsworth, who was Chief Justice of the Supreme Court. Again, disaster struck. Judge Collingsworth, in a spell of intoxication plunged overboard from a ship in Galveston bay. Robert Wilson, a member of the Senate, was then put forth, but Lamar was elected with 6,695 votes to only 252 for Wilson, a complete rout for the Houston faction.[7]

Rusk's oft-expressed desire to return to his home, his family and his law practice was still delayed by the call of his beloved country. While he was still engaged in the Indian wars, Congress elected him Chief Justice of the Supreme Court of the

5Telegraph and Texas Register, May 23, 1838.
6Ibid.
7Lubbock, p. 82.

Republic to fill the vacancy resulting from the suicide of Chief Justice James T. Collingsworth during his candidacy for President.

Rusk's election occured February 3, 1839, while he was still involved in the Indian wars. Due to the general turmoil that year, Rusk as well as the associate judges were busy in other affairs and no session of the court was held in 1839. Judge Collingsworth had not convened the court before his death so it evolved that Rusk held the first session of the Texas Supreme Court.

Under the Constitution, the court consisted of the Chief Justice and the District Judges of the nation. The court opened in Austin January 13, 1840. The District Judges in attendance were A. B. Shelby, William J. Jones, John T. Mills and John Hemphill. The courthouse was a residence owned by Major Asa Brigham "in the lower part of Austin."[8] Some historians discount the importance of Rusk's service on the Supreme bench. Hemphill, who was a member of the panel and later served as Chief Justice, remarked: "As a Judge, his career was too brief to form an important feature in the figure of his life," but added that "in the consultation room and in his opinions, he gave abundant evidence of capacities for high judicial eminence."[9]

The decisions handed down by Judge Rusk "do not display great learning . . . but it is to be recollected, that during the first two terms of the Supreme Court of the United States all the judges did not write half so much. The Chief Justice proved himself adequate to the times; if in his sententious opinions, he quoted no authorities, he displayed more wisdom that some of the fellows, who quoted from schools and systems which had never been introduced in Texas."[10]

Looking back 85 years over the history of jurisprudence in Texas, Stayton in his article in the *Texas Law Review* in 1925 is inclined to attach greater importance to Rusk's service in the single term of the Supreme Court. Forty-nine cases were disposed of during the term that lasted four and a half months. Most of the opinions were on question of jurisdiction or practice and all were short, averaging less than two pages. Chief Jus-

---

[8]Stayton, p. 16.
[9]Hemphill.
[10]**Texas Almanac Compendium**, pp. 64-65.

tice Rusk and Judge Jones handed down five opinions each. Rusk's were the soul of brevity, averaging less than a page, and were for the most part, "as plain and bare as a trial court's judgment."[11]

Some of his opinions were cited in courts even down to recent times. Stayton adds that Rusk "deserves the credit of having gotten the court started and having cleared his docket of all the cases that were ready for trial."[12] Having completed the term of court, Rusk resigned June 1, 1840, and returned to his family and his law practice in Nacogdoches.

---

[11]Stayton, p. 16.
[12]Ibid., pp. 16-17.

CHAPTER 20

Halcyon Days in Nacogdoches

Having discharged his military obligations and completed his service as Chief Justice, it was with a feeling of satisfaction that Rusk resumed the practice of law. To be at home again with his family, to live with his neighbors, to walk the streets of his home town in the role of a private citizen, to sit with clients and friends in his office brought a fulfillment which had been long delayed.

During the first few years in Nacogdoches, the Rusk family lived in what was called the "Red House," an adobe and frame structure on the main plaza of the town. It had been built by Col. Jose de las Piedras and occupied by him during his tenure as commander of the garrison at Nacogdoches from 1828 until he was driven out with his troops by the Texans in the Battle of Nacogdoches in 1832.[1]

As a site for a permanent family home and plantation, Rusk bought in 1841 what was known as the "Santo Domingo Rancho," on the North Road, half a mile from town.[2] On this site, Rusk built a modest home which he and his family occupied until the time of his death. It was described as a "double pen" log house, by F. I. Tucker, attorney, pioneer resident of Nacogdoches and authority on local history. It was of a traditional type of architecture of the time, two large squares composing the wings, with hall or breeze-way between, shed rooms on the back and porch on the front. Tucker remembered playing in the old house as a small boy after it was abandoned.[3] An old picture shows the dwelling with white lumber siding, which must have been added after the house was first built.

Today the site is occupied by the Redeemer Lutheran Church and Student Center. It is on a gentle hill which overlooks the beautiful campus of Stephen F. Austin State University, part of which was formerly included in the Rusk planta-

[1]Blount, 184.
[2]**Ibid.**, also Deed Records, County Clerk's Office, Nacogdoches.
[3]Interview by author with F. I. Tucker, 1969.

tion. Lofty pines now grace the land which Rusk's slaves once tended as fields and pastures. It was said that the statesman-farmer could sit on his front porch and watch the field hands at work. However, the evidence is that he spent little time porch-sitting. If he had leisure time, it was spent in his library with shelves of books. A nephew, John Rusk, said, long after the statesman's death, that he seldom remembered seeing Uncle Tom without a book in his hand, and that children playing around him never disturbed his reading.[4]

In February, 1841, the year Rusk bought Santo Domingo Rancho, he entered a law partnership with J. Pinckney Henderson of San Augustine, a lawyer who had arrived in Texas just after the Battle of San Jacinto. Announcement of the partnership was made in the San Augustine *Journal and Advertiser* of March 2, 1841:

> "*Rusk & Henderson, Attorneys & Counsellers at Law.*
> "*Having* resumed the practice and entered into co-partnership, will attend the Circuit Courts of the fifth, sixth and seventh Judicial Districts of this Republic, and such other courts in the adjoining districts, as their arrangements will enable them to do, together with the Supreme Court. Their partnership does not include the county of Houston, but they will both attend that court.
>   "T. J. Rusk, Nacogdoches
>   "J. Pinckney Henderson,
>   San Augustine"

The firm was highly successful and well respected. The partners seldom lost a case, particularly where criminal charges such as murder were involved. Besides the reward of being free of public pressure and following the profession which he loved, Rusk had the satisfaction of being able to make payments to some of his creditors back in Georgia who had dogged him since he came to Texas. But it was several years before he was to be free from debt.

Adolphus Sterne, a Jewish German national, Texas booster, sometime Alcalde and later Postmaster of Nacogdoches, kept a criptic diary of doings in Nacogdoches from 1838 to 1851, a valuable contribution to history. He was an admirer of Rusk, the town's most distinguished citizen, and made frequent entries of the General's activites. Among other matters, he mentioned

---

[4]Blount, 186, quoting John Rusk of Nacogdoches, son of David Rusk.

Rusk's trips to court in the various county seats of East Texas, murder trials, speeches, social affairs, community services and one quarrel.

On April 16, 1841, he recorded "General Rusk returned from Red River County this Evening . . . Rusk much improved in appearance—good. . . ." On October, 22, 1841: "Several gentlemen Delegates arrived on their way to Austin, had a very fine Party . . . Gels Rusk and Houston and Lady eta all there. . . ."[5]

November 18: "Rawles and others were put upon their trial today, for hanging willis, the Horse thief. Duffield, Rusk, Burke, Jenning, and Wm. K. Scurry made eloquent speachez. Court adjourned until tomorrow." Next day he wrote: "Trial of Rawls et all was went into again this morning:—they were all acquitted."

March 26, 1842: "a meeting at the Court House took place to day, a great many persons present, general Rusk addressed the meeting in a very eloquent manner, a set of Resolutions drafted by Gel R. were adopted."

April 14: "very cold this morning—to wet to plough—planted Sweet Potatoe slips, worked in the garden, interpreted between General Rusk & Jose Ma Mora respecting a suit Mora is about to institute against J. J. Simpson & Wm Simpson. Gel Rusk promised me half of the fee if he gains the suit—which is one fourth of the land. . . ."

May 10: "our District Court in session—the case of the Republic vs Borroughs came up for killing of McKeever of Crockett hard work to get a jury— . . . the case took all day and most of the Bar made speeches, gel Rusk concluding against the Prisoner, but his argument was more of a Cast, to acquit, than to bring the man guilty, I believe it is the first time he has taken part in the Prosecution of a Criminal offense where death would be the Penalty if the Accused would be found guilty—he merely expounded the Law but did not *appeal* to the feelings of the jury which he is so capable of doing & which no doubt he would have done on the other side of the question—he done his duty and no more—the jury retired at 8½ P. M. returned at

---

[5]McDonald, Archie P., Ed. **Hurrah for Texas! The Diary of Adolphus Sterne** (Texian Press, Waco, 1969). Sterne, like many of his contemporaries wrote without aid of punctuation. The excerpts quoted here are from McDonald's edited version.

10 P. M. verdict not guilty, a thing devoutly hoped for by every one."

Not guilty seemed to be the usual verdict in other criminal cases in the same court session as recorded in Sterne's diary. Rusk was involved as an attorney in most of the cases.

June 28: "Militia paraded, quota of volunteers required by secy. of war in this county. Rusk and others spoke. all hands drunk this evening yet not one fight occured during the day."

Similar entries, giving impressions and events, typical of the era and revealing as to General Rusk's life at this period abound in the diary. One wry note—August 29, 1842, "Judge Taylor & gen Rusk fell out and made friends again, the Cause of the quarrell was—*whiskey* & Taylor was in the wrong." The diarist didn't say who drank the liquor; possibly both.

Wedding bells for General Rusk's younger brother—January 26, 1843: "David Rusk is to be married to night, all hands gone out to John Reids the Bride's Fathers House." Then on the next day, January 27: "Gel Rusk gives a Ball this evening the hole world is invited—went with my wife & Eugenia of *course*, staid till one A. M. . . . went to bed tired to death and tired of frolics."

A tragedy involved Rusk's law partner. Sterne entered in his diary November 3, 1842: "Eastern Mail arrived, brought the intelligence that Gen. Henderson had killed N. P. Garner of San Augustin, send Gel Rusk to go & defend him." Following an examining trial, Henderson was placed in custody of the sheriff. Then, on November 28, Sterne wrote: "Gen. Rusk returned from San Augustine. Henderson got discharged honorably, good, very good."

Henderson was a cultured man and it was a tragedy that he should be forced into such an affair. It was a part of the violent times then prevailing in Texas.

"I had been annoyed for more than a year by a desperado named N. B. Garner whom I was at last forced to Slay," Henderson wrote to Dr. Ashbel Smith. "He had often threatened to kill me and twice when I was unarmed attempted to assassinate me. I had a great abhorance of the shedding of human blood in a street fight and laboured to avoid it. . . . A few days before I killed Garner he waylaid me with a double barreled gun to assassinate me as I passed but I learned his movements & avoided him—from that time I *marked* him as my own.

106

"He was preparing to shoot me when I shot him and was closely watching an opportunity to take some advantage of me for he was a coward and would not attack me with pistols when I was similarly armed. . . . I regret that the *beast forced* me to do that which some ruffian ought to have done but I shall never regret that I killed him as I am sure he then would have killed me if I had not slain him. . . . I demanded an investigation of the affair . . . & the court of inquiry declared me fully justified."[6]

[6]Ashbel Smith Papers, Henderson to Ashbel Smith, Nov. 25, 1842.

CHAPTER 21

The Two Generals Battle With Words

Rusk responded to the call of Congress in 1843 for a second tour of duty as Major General in command of the militia. His tenure was short, there was no combat, but the assignment brought on an angry clash between Rusk and President Houston. It was during Houston's second administration. Mexico was still claiming Texas and making hit-and-run forays across the Rio Grande, even capturing San Antonio on two occasions in 1842.

Congress passed a bill for the protection of the western and southwestern frontier. The act provided for the election of a major general and required him to call up immediately six companies of militia. It also specified that, "should the major-general of the militia deem it expedient, he may at any time take the field, and command . . . any number of troops."[1]

President Houston vetoed the bill as it divested him of authority over the militia. He also feared that it would break up negotiations which he was carrying on with Santa Anna for a peaceful settlement. Congress promptly passed the bill over the veto and proceeded to elect Rusk as Major General on January 16, 1843. It was the same situation over again as when Congress had overridden a veto in Houston's first administration in 1837 and had named Rusk as Major General. It caused some bitter words between old friends—Rusk and Houston.

It was six weeks after Rusk's election by Congress when the President signed the Major General's commission on March 2, 1843,[2] but it was in May when Rusk actually received the certification.[3] Meanwhile, on February 2, Rusk had written a letter to the editor of the *Western Advocate*, saying: "I am aware that in accepting the office . . . I am taking upon myself a weighty responsibility; I am also satisfied that his Excellency

---

[1]Yoakum, II, p. 385.
[2]Copy of Commission in 'Special Collections, Stephen F. Austin State University Library.
[3]Sterrett, p. 108.

will, as usual with him, throw obstacles in the way of a faithful discharge of the duties which devolve upon me. . . ."[4]

Whether Rusk intended the letter for publication is uncertain, but it *was* published, not only in the *Advocate,* but was copied in the Houston *Morning Star* on May 11 and stirred a hornet's nest. Houston was quick to demand an explanation.

"The expressions imputed to you in relation to myself are so much at variance with the sentiments expressed to me in your letter of a date but little different, that I cannot but bring them into vivid contrast," Houston wrote in a long letter to Rusk on May 13. "And it is impossible for me to arrive at any agreeable conclusion. I say so, because I am unconscious of ever having thrown any obstacles in the way of a faithful discharge of any duties devolving on you."[5]

Referring to a statement in Rusk's published letter that he (Rusk) would never shelter himself "as the President has heretofore done, from crossing the enemy's boundary line under a doctrine which has been so fully exploded in our mother country," Houston denied any such doctrine on his part, but declared it would be unconstitutional in Texas to take the militia into foreign territory.

Concluding his letter, the President expressed the hope that Rusk could explain his position, "render such reasons as will satisfy my mind that you have not been united with persons who are endeavoring to foment dissention in the country— embarrass the Executive in the discharge of his duties, and subvert our institutions as well as all civil rule and public order."[6]

This last remark was an unkind blow, but Houston expended his bitterest sarcasm in a letter to their mutual friend, Dr. Robert A. Irion, of Nacogdoches:

> "We hear that General Rusk is soon to be on the march with the advance of the 'grande armie,' *for the reduction of the palaces of the Montezumas!* This is awful! It cannot be under the law of the last session of Congress. It must be gratuitous as I presume. . . . I am well assured that the General never intended his letter for publication. He may well exclaim, 'save me from my friends,' &c, &c. It will be very apt to cause a 'tall spree.' I pity Rusk. He has certainly fallen upon evil companionship, and will

[4]**Morning Star** (Houston) May 11, 1843.
[5]Rusk Papers, Houston to Rusk, May 10, 1843.
[6]**Ibid.**

repent when it is too late. You know I have been much inclined to like Rusk; and could have done so, only that I could not confide in his firmness and stability. In these qualities he is so defective that I do candidly believe the man cannot be honest, even if his heart is so inclined. To me he is a problem. Like the ass between the stacks of hay, his neutral attitude has created for him a sort of negative character which by toleration he enjoys, and by common consent his vices and his habits are permitted to pass unnoticed. Those who look upon him indulge in the passing remark that 'Rusk is a good fellow—I like him—he is his own worst enemy'. . . ."[7]

Obviously the criticisms were extreme and, for the most part, unjust. The attack was in keeping with Houston's usual attitude that anyone who opposed him was a contemptible rascal. On many other occasions, both before and after this tiff, Houston had generous praise for Rusk.

Finally when Rusk was able to procure a copy of the bill passed by Congress creating his office as well as his official Commission from President Houston, he set about organizing the militia. He gave orders to the Brigadier Generals of the first, second and third brigades requiring them to organize their units. In spite of the earlier rebuff, he wrote the President asking his opinion about an expedition against Mexico as a reprisal for encroachments of the Mexicans and their atrocities against the Texas people.

Houston dashed off a sharp reply: "You ask whether my sanction will be given for the militia to advance upon the Rio Grande and attack the enemy. The law under which you were appointed does not embrace the subject of invasion, but simply of *protection*. It surely cannot be imagined that our legislators designed . . . to make the agent . . . a 'law unto himself,' controlled by nothing but *his own will*. . . . The words 'invasion' or 'foreign war' no where appear in the enactment."[8]

Though General Rusk had predicted at the time of his appointment that President Houston would throw obstacles in the way of carrying out his mission, he nevertheless had avowed his determination "to use my utmost exertions to defend the country against its enemies, and, as far as possible, to avenge the insults and injuries which . . . have been heaped upon us by

---

[7]Houston's **Writings**, IV, pp. 202-03, Houston to Dr. R. A. Irion.
[8]Letter Book No. 40, Houston to Rusk, May 31, 1843, Texas State Library.

110

Mexico."[9]   However, Houston won the tilt.   Rusk resigned in June and returned to his law practice in Nacogdoches—always a place of refuge when his public services were no longer needed or desired.   This marked the end of his military career, but he was to be known through the rest of his life by the title, "General."

Being of sensitive nature, Rusk was deeply hurt by Houston's attack, but he was not one to hold a grudge.   A few years later, he assisted Houston in his campaign for nomination for the presidency of the United States.   For his part, Houston continued friendly and solicitous in their personal relations.   Hear him speaking years later in their old hometown, Nacogdoches: ". . . who was it for twelve years stood by me shoulder to shoulder in the Senate struggling for the good of Texas? General Rusk assisted in that hurculean task which gave Texas millions of money and reserved her public lands.   Would that he were here to answer for me!"[10]

However, relations between Rusk and Houston were still strained as the time approached for the presidential election of 1844.   Political maneuvers were under way a full year before the election.   Under the Constitution, Houston was not eligible to succeed himself.   Dr. Anson Jones, Secretary of State in the Houston Cabinet, was itching for the honor but, as in past elections, "everybody was waiting to see what Thomas J. Rusk would do."[11]

Possibly there was a shade of jealousy in Jones' expressed opinion that Rusk had "neither the learning, the application nor the character to do credit to the place."   Later he conceded that Rusk "has more talent than I had given him credit for," but feared "it is all for Demagougeism, cunning & treachery."[12]

James Webb, formerly Attorney General under Lamar, wanted to run, but hesitated.   "Houston is tottering on his throne," he believed, "but if he can by any means, bring to his aid the popularity and influence of Rusk, he is safe.   He may go on . . . & set the Constitution, laws & every thing else in defiance, & laugh at those who oppose his high-handed lawlessness."[13]   Houston kept silent but apparently favored Jones.

---

[9]**Morning Star**, May 11, 1843.
[10]Houston's **Writings**, VI, speech at Nacogdoches, July 9, 1859.
[11]Gambrell, **Anson Jones**, p. 285.
[12]**Ibid.**, p. 204.
[13]**Ibid.**

Well in advance of the election, conventions were held in counties throughout the Republic. An enthusiastic gathering in Nacogdoches nominated Rusk and almost every county in East Texas followed suit.

There seems little doubt that Rusk, for the second time in Texas history, could have had the presidency if he had so desired. Political factions at the time were divided roughly on the line of Houston versus Lamar, or Houston and anti-Houston. Rusk could have been elected by either faction as there was no candidate of near his strength and popularity to oppose him. However, if he had chosen to run, he might have avoided factionalism and striven for harmony and the healing of wounds for the welfare of Texas.

This was the note sounded at the county convention at Crockett, one of the first to nominate Rusk. He was hailed as the man "best calculated to unite and reduce into one the many conflicting interests of our country, as well as to heal the innumerable existing feelings of bitter sectional and party prejudices."[14]

Both Lamar and Houston, titular heads of the two main factions, were Rusk's old friends from war days, in spite of occasional rifts, and Rusk would not have hurt either for his own personal glory. Possibly this might have influenced his decision. Anyway, in August, 1843, Rusk definitely declined to be a candidate. Anson Jones need wait no longer. He entered the race and defeated Gen. Edward Burleson in the election, September 2, 1844.

Jones and Rusk seldom saw eye-to-eye. Neither quite trusted the other. The Jones administration was short, as annexation was soon to be achieved, an event which marked the end of Jones' political career. For Rusk, it was the beginning of his most notable service for Texas.

---

[14]**Redlander** (San Augustine), Dec. 22, 1842.

CHAPTER 22

"Eyes of the Civilized World Are Upon Us"

From the time Texas won its independence from Mexico, there had been a desire on the part of the people for annexation to the United States. In fact, in the very first election in the new Republic in September, 1836, the voters almost unanimously favored union with the states in which most of them had originated. However, the proposal was rejected in Washington, and Texas proved that it could work out its own destiny. The greatest factor in the rejection by the United States was the slavery issue, the northern states objecting to the addition of slave territory.

However, when Great Britain showed a desire of gaining influence in Texas and Mexico to the threat of American interest, President John Tyler became concerned and a treaty of annexation was negotiated, only to be rejected by the United States Senate in 1844. The matter became an issue in the next presidential campaign and James Polk, who favored annexation, was elected. Before he took office, a joint resolution in Congress offered to receive Texas into the Union.

Meanwhile, Texas representatives had negotiated a preliminary peace treaty with Mexico, who had never acknowledged Texas independence. Mexico had warned earlier that annexation would be equivalent to a declaration of war. Now Texas had a choice of a treaty with Mexico and a promise of peace or annexation and almost certain war. The decision was prompt and emphatic. The Texas Senate unanimously rejected the treaty with Mexico on June 21, 1845. Two days later, both houses of the Texas Congress voted unanimously for annexation. A convention to complete the process of union and to draft a state constitution was called to meet July 4.

The Convention of 1845 brought together most of the great men of Texas. It was generally conceded to have been the ablest body ever assembled in Texas—at least up to that time. Only Sam Houston was missing. He had been elected

113

a delegate from Montgomery County (Conroe) but for some obscure reason failed to appear and his seat was filled by an alternate.

Thomas J. Rusk was one of the delegates from Nacogdoches County. He acted as chairman of an informal meeting on the day prior to the opening of the session. His experience in the Convention of 1836 in completing the Constitution of the Republic and his services as Chief Justice of the Supreme Court made him the logical man to whom the assembly could turn for leadership.

When the session opened on the morning of July 4, 1845, H. G. Runnels nominated Rusk for President of the Convention. There were no other nominations and Rusk was unanimously elected. On this occasion, he was not reluctant to accept the assignment which afforded him the opportunity for one of his greatest services to Texas. His responsibility was to guide the process of annexation and to preside over the task of writing a constitution acceptable to both the people of Texas and the Government of the United States.

"The object for which we have assembled deeply interests the people of Texas. We have the hopes of our present population, as well as the millions who may come after us, in our hands; the eyes of the civilized world are upon us," declared Rusk in addressing the Convention on that momentous day which significantly was the anniversary of American independence. "The history of the world may be searched in vain for a parallel to the present instance of two governments amalgamating themselves into one from a pure devotion to that great principle that man, by enlightening his intellect and cultivating those moral sentiments with which God has impressed him, is capable of self-government."[1]

Continuing his address to the delegates, Rusk said the terms of annexation "are honorable alike to the United States and to Texas. . . . I would not seek to alter the terms proposed by the government of the United States." He concluded:

> "Texas, animated by the same spirit and following the bright example of the fathers of the American Revolution has acquired at the cost of blood, her freedom and independence from those who would have enslaved her people. She now, with a unanimity unparalleled, enters that

---

[1]Lubbock, pp. 171-72.

114

great confederacy to whose keeping the bright jewel of human liberty is confided, content to bear the burdens and share the benefits which republican government carries in her train."[2]

As president of the Convention, Rusk presented the annexation documents which he had received from President Anson Jones and assigned a committee of 15 delegates to draw up a resolution accepting the United States offer of annexation. The committee reported the same day with a resolution of acceptance which was adopted by a vote of 55 to one, with five delegates not voting. When the result was announced, "the delegates stood up and shouted in a long, moist-eyed demonstration of joy."[3]

Rusk presented a certified copy of the ordinance to the American charge d'affaires in Texas, Andrew Jackson Donelson, who gave assurance that "From the date of this ordinance Texas will have acquired the right to the protection of the United States, and . . . the President of the United States has taken steps to afford . . . protection in the most effective manner against future Mexican and Indian invasion."[4]

Annexation of Texas was a blow to radical abolitionists in the United States who advocated destruction of slavery at once. However, some of the more moderate anti-slavery advocates realized the importance of securing the vast Texas territory and were willing to accept it, slavery and all.

There were also a few in Texas who were not enthusiastic about annexation and might have leaned toward the alternative of casting Texas' lot with Great Britain and Mexico. Rusk, among others, suspected President Anson Jones of being opposed to the union. J. Pinckney Henderson, Rusk's law partner, feared "The President is not as *anxious* as some of us are to see the measure consumated, but . . . will carry out the wishes of the people. . . . If the President is opposed to our wishes, this is a bad time to excite him or punish him . . . rather let us *coax* him on."[5]

Rusk favored dissolving the Jones administration and setting up a provisional government to conclude the annexation as he did not trust Jones. The matter was solved by the Con-

[2]Ibid., p. 172.
[3]Wisehart, p. 484.
[4]Lubbock, p. 174.
[5]Gambrell, **Anson Jones,** p. 406.

vention ordering the exact steps to be followed by President Jones in completing the merger. Rusk was accused by the Jones forces—with good reason—of being back of a plan to oust the President. As a matter of fact, Rusk and a few others continued their opposition to Jones throughout the Convention.

For his part, when all was done, Jones boasted: "I won independence and annexation of my country. If I am wrong in any particular, let the records of my negotiation show it."[6] Lubbock comments that "Nevertheless, President Jones was ruined politically by the suspicion that he had opposed annexation. . . ."[7] Later, Jones coveted Rusk's seat in the United States Senate but was disappointed.

With the formalities of annexation completed, except for formal approval by the people, the Convention turned its attention to the more arduous task of writing the Constitution for the new State. To expedite the work, President Rusk appointed five committees: One on the State of the Nation, a separate committee on each of the three branches of government—executive, legislative and judicial—and one on general provisions of the Constitution.[8]

Rusk did not confine his services to presiding over the assembly, but entered into the discussions and debates over crucial issues. He would call one of the delegates to the chair while he took the floor to express his views, and he recorded his vote on the important decisions. With so many great men with differing interests and opinions, there were long and sometimes bitter debates and it taxed Rusk's best talents to maintain a degree of peace and harmony.

Some wanted to allow the Legislature to override a governor's veto by a simple majority, but Rusk argued for the two-thirds rule. "The people are governed too much; there are too many laws," he said, sounding a familiar note heard down to the present time. He argued against and defeated a proposal to have the Secretary of State elected by popular vote rather than being appointed by the Governor.

Rusk took an active part in debates on the Judiciary System, which he considered the most important branch of the Government. He lost in his efforts for longer terms for su-

[6]Lubbock, p. 174.
[7]Ibid., p. 175.
[8]Barker, History, p. 391.

preme and district court judges, which were placed at six years, and was only partly successful in his efforts for higher salaries for judges. The pay was finally set at not less than $2,000 a year for supreme court judges and not less than $1,750 for district judges.[9]

Conflicting interests of the different regions of the State and as between farming areas with their slaves and cities with transient populations flared in the debate over the basis of representation in the State Legislature. To settle the dispute, President Rusk appointed a committee to work out a solution. The result, finally adopted by the Convention, based representation in the House on "free population" and in the Senate on "qualified electors."

Rusk opposed "conscientious scruples" as an excuse from military service, arguing that such a principle would "strike directly at the foundations of government," and if such had prevailed with the majority of the people of Texas "we should not have been in existence as a Republic." However, he failed to carry his point.[10] Another disputed matter was a provision barring ministers from seats in the Legislature, some claiming that such would be a violation of the principle of separation of church and state. Rusk contended that ministers should have the same privilege of serving in office as other citizens, but again was overruled.

One of the distinctive features of the Texas Constitution of 1845 was the homestead act which exempted ones home and certain other property from seizure for payment of debt. As introduced by the committee, this article exempted not to exceed 160 acres of land. Rusk left the chair and offered an amendment to increase the exemption to not more than 200 acres of land. After some debate, the amendment was adopted and this enactment became one of the enduring laws of Texas, handed down to the present time.

Some of Rusk's arguments on this issue seem quaint and naive today: "I believe that the credit system is a great injury to any country, and is productive of very little good," he declared in response to objections that the homestead law would injure credit. (He spoke as one who was troubled most of his life by debts.) "This country must be an agricultural

---

[9]Ibid., pp. 292,300.
[10]Stayton, p. 19.

country," he proclaimed—a pronouncement which was to hold true for many decades. "To develop its resources we ought to give permanence to the titles of the individuals who occupy the soil. We ought to place them beyond the reach of any contengencies arising from misfortune or mismanagement."[11]

Location of the capital, bone of contention since the birth of the Republic, brought on a lively dispute. The matter was finally settled along lines proposed by Rusk. Austin was to be the seat of government until 1850, at which time an election would be held and the city receiving the majority of votes would be the capital until 1870.[12]

After laboring through 56 hot days of July and August, the Convention ended on a note of harmony and patriotic sentiment. President Rusk was voted unanimously a resolution of thanks for the "promptness, fidelity and inpartiality with which he had discharged his arduous and responsible duties."[13]

Rusk was deeply moved by the acclaim of the delegates with whom he had worked so earnestly through the long, hot summer. Responding to the resolution, he spoke with restrained emotion:

> "I shall cherish it, gentlemen, as long as life shall last with me, and transmit it to my children as a bright inheritance which the poor services of their father little merited. . . . The proceedings of this convention, I think I may safely say without vanity or any undue prejudice in favor of Texas, our adopted land, may well compare with those of any similar body which has met within the last hundred years. . . ."

Rusk closed with an appeal for harmony in the new state and the hope that when the Constitution went into effect,

> ". . . the angry passions attendant upon political dissensions will be hushed, that all sectional feelings and jealousies, and the strife of personal ambitions will cease, and that for many long years to come it [the Constitution] will continue the organic law of a people united as a band of brothers, animated by the best feeling of the human

[11]Ibid., p. 20.
[12]Middleton, Annie Irene, The Texas Convention of 1845. in Southwestern Historical Quarterly, XXV, p. 346.
[13]Ibid., pp. 332-33.

heart, and prompted in action by that pure and lively patriotism which has characterized Texas thus far."[14]

The Texas State Constitution was a charter of which the Convention delegates could indeed be proud. Even Daniel Webster, who was no friend of Texas, said it was the best State constitution ever written. It was the basic law of Texas up to the Civil War. Conclusion of the memorable assembly was an occasion for celebration on the part of the delegates, and for Rusk the festivities brought on a sad anti-climax to the great service he had just achieved.

"The Convention adjourned yesterday and most of them are gone. Genl. Rusk is here on a big spree and has been for two days," Dr Moses Johnson of Independence wrote his wife. And William B. Ochiltree reported: "I left Rusk in Crockett on *one grand spree.*"[15]

The new Constitution, along with the question of annexation, was submitted to the people October 10, 1845, and both were overwhelmingly approved by the voters. President Polk in Washington affixed his signature to a bill extending the laws of the United States over Texas. The State Government was installed February 16, 1846, with J. Pinckney Henderson as Governor. The Lone Star flag was replaced by the Stars and Stripes.

By a remarkable coincidence, the annexation proceedings brought about a renewal, after some 15 years of Rusk's friendship with his old South Carolina benefactor, John C. Calhoun. The great Southern statesman was now Secretary of State in the cabinet of President Tyler. Rusk sent him a certified copy of the resolutions of the convention, expressing gratitude to Calhoun for the service he had rendered in espousing the cause of Texas.

"I accept this highly honorable approval of the distinguished body over which you [Rusk] presided, of the part I performed towards the consumation of this great measure, with sincere pleasure and gratitude," Calhoun wrote in a personal letter to Rusk. "Taken altogether, it is one of the most memorable events of our history; and I am proud to have my name associated with it. . . .

"I avail myself of the occasion to tender to you my

---

[14]**Ibid.,** pp. 758-59.
[15]Gambrell, **Anson Jones,** p. 412.

congratulations at the high honor conferred on you by the convention, in selecting you to preside over its deliberations. It is indeed, a striking, and to me gratifying coincidence, that an old acquaintance, and law student of mine, and native of the same district with myself should be chairman and organ of the committee by which it was consumated."[16]

Such words from his old friend and benefactor must have warmed the heart of Thomas J. Rusk. The renewal of his friendship with one of the great men of the South was indeed a rewarding experience.

[16]Niles' **National Register,** Oct. 18, 1845.

CHAPTER 23

"An Acknowledged Power in the Land"

In the prime of his life at 42, Thomas J. Rusk went home to Nacogdoches after presiding over the Convention of 1845 where the benediction was said for the bold Texas Republic. He had seen its birth and its demise and could vision now its rebirth as a bright star in the galaxy of American states. The career of Rusk falls roughly into three decades: First, the period of his law-practice and business activities in Georgia, then his service for the Republic and, finally his brilliant career in the Senate of the United States.

Between the latter two periods was a brief interlude in his hometown with his family and kindly friends and neighbors. Nacogdoches was not a community of wealth—the more prosperous folk now lived in San Augustine—but there was a society of great Texans in the historic old town. Many of the men were veterans of the Revolution and Indian wars and several were signers of the Declaration of Independence.

"Colonel Frost Thorn and lady were esteemed among the leaders of those who dispensed princely hospitality. Their entertainments were graced by the presence of youth, beauty and talent." It was a democratic society but it is interesting to observe from writers and journalists of the time that everyone of importance bore a title: General, Colonel, Doctor or Judge. Apparently there were few Captains and no Lieutenants or Sergeants. The people of East Texas were the controlling element in the affairs of the country. "The power that these men wielded in the political life of the Republic is shown by the fact that they organized almost every congress that was assembled during the decade of its existence."[1]

Among the distinguished citizens of Nacogdoches listed by John S. Ford were Col. James Reiley, Gen. James S. Mayfield, Dr. James Starr, Col. John Forbes, Gen. Hayden Edwards, Col. Thomas J. Jennings, Col. Adolphus Sterne, Col. J. S. Rob-

[1]Barker, **Texas History,** p. 396.

erts and Henry Reguet.[2] To these must be added Dr. Robert A. Irion, Charles S. Taylor, Kelsey H. Douglass, Amos Clark and William Clark, as mentioned by Eugene C. Barker.[3]

John S. Ford, himself prominent, lived in San Augustine as did Rusk's law partners, J. Pinckney Henderson and Kenneth L. Anderson. Here also were Sam Houston, George W. Terrell, John A. Greer, Joseph Rowe, William R. Scurry, William B. Ochiltree, B. Rush Wallace, Oran M. Roberts (later governor), Royal T. Wheeler, Henry W. Sublett and Richard S. Walker.

If this array of distinguished men and their families formed an East Texas "aristocracy", it was a nobility of deeds and service and not of wealth and heritage. They, with others of their breed in other parts of Texas, were aptly described by Ford as the "old timers who had done duty on the skirmish line of civilization."[4]

In reciting his list of prominent men of Nacogdoches Ford declared: "General Rusk stood first among them. He was an acknowledged power in the land—a ruler in Israel. The lawyer, the statesman, the general, the patriotic citizen, the steadfast friend had the heart-felt esteem of all who knew him."[5]

Yet, with all this esteem, with honors which had been showered upon him, with success he had achieved and with the love and respect of his family, there was a note of despondency about Rusk at this time. Friends, conscious of their own weaknesses, could forgive such faults as he had, but seemingly he could not forgive himself. Possibly he suffered remorse from his drinking bout at the close of the Convention in Austin. Seemingly, too, his health at this time was poor. His feelings are revealed in a missive of advice which he wrote for his four sons, February 22, 1846:

> "To Benjn. L., John C., Cicero and Tho. D. Rusk:
> "Knowing the great uncertainty of life and the absolute certainty of death, and feeling that my frame is giving way, I have thought it would perhaps not be amiss for me to address a few words to that famiiy with which it has pleased God to bless me and which at my death, I must leave behind me.

---

[2]Ford, p. 17.
[3]Barker, **Texas History**, p. 396.
[4]Ford, p. 56.
[5]**Ibid.**, p. 17.

"I have had my share of trouble in this world and the most which I have suffered has proceed from three causes:

1st Getting in debt.
2nd Becoming Security for others.
3rd Intemperance.

These three courses are the rocks upon which I have wrecked most of my earthly happiness and which I would warn my sons against. Debt beyond the means of paying, to a sensitive mind, is perfect slavery and will eventually destroy the brightest intellect. It cramps and destroys the best feelings of human nature and added to intemperance will make earth a hell. I trust my sons will read over the lines I have traced here and repeat them whenever tempted to go in debt beyond their certain means of paying, go security for anyone or drinking ardent spirits. The habit of drinking is easily formed and almost impossible to break. I trust when I have gone from them they will act with correctness and prudence and see that their mother spends her days in comfort and plenty, cost what exertions on their part it may.

"Be industrious, honest, sober, kind to the unfortunate and distressed. Speak evil of none and associate only with those of principles and reputation and you will then be in the right road to the only true happiness which the earth affords and I trust that God will bless and prosper you long after the hand which traced these lines shall lay cold and powerless in the grave. 22nd February.

"Tho. J. Rusk."[6]

At the foot of his father's message, possibly at some later date, the youngest son, Thomas David, inscribed a pledge:

"The hand of affection traced the above lines and it would be almost sacerlize [sic] to depart from the course pointed out for us to follow. Why should we not follow the advice. Is it wise to dash from our lips the cup of happiness and substitute that of misery. I make this resolve to follow it at whatever cost. Whatever exertion is necessary to guard, protect and provide for that mother who watched over me when unable to protect myself shall be used, and as long as I live, she shall need nothing, and my father I shall try and repay in some measure for the trouble and anxiety he has had in teaching me to pursue the path of honor and virtue.

"DR"[7]

---

[6]Rusk Papers, endorsed "Advice to my children", Feb. 22, 1846.
[7]Ibid.

Rusk was elected United States Senator by the First Texas Legislature on February 21. Due to slow communications at the time, it is quite unlikely that he had received word of this honor at the time he wrote the message to his sons on February 22.

As was the case during most of his life, Rusk was having personal and financial problems. His father, John Rusk, died in South Carolina in 1844 and was buried in the churchyard of the Old Stone Church which he had built. After his death, Thomas J. and David Rusk assumed almost the entire responsibility for the support of their mother. They urged her to join them in Texas, but she refused, probably baffled by the prospect of the long journey and the wild reputation of the faraway land. At one time, Thomas J. and his wife, Mary, journeyed to South Carolina to visit the mother, whose name also was Mary.[8] Letters among the Rusk papers reveal that the two sons were solicitous of their mother's welfare, kept in touch with her and sent her money from time to time.

Rusk was still plagued by old debts. His salary had gone unpaid for much of his public service. He never acquired wealth. Such property as he had was in slaves and land, neither of which was very profitable nor could readily be turned into cash. It might be said that he was "land poor." The year he arrived in Texas (1835) he received one league of land as his headright. To this was added in 1838 a labor of land under new headright policies. He also received grants amounting to 1,600 acres for his military service and acquired other acreages either by purchase, trades or legal fees. By the time of his death in 1857 he had accumulated a large acreage in tracts scattered through many Texas counties, but still his cash assets were small.[9]

Rusk and Sam Houston were again on cordial terms. Houston and his recent bride, Margaret Lea, were living in San Augustine, possibly for the best. The blue-eyed Anna Raguet, whom Houston had courted, had married Dr. Robert A. Irion of Nacogdoches, Houston's friend, physician and bearer of love messages to Miss Anna.

In spite of the fact that Margaret supposedly had persuaded Houston to give up drink and Rusk was struggling to

---

[8]Blount, p. 189.
[9]Records in State Land Office, Austin, and County Clerk's Office, Nacogdoches.

throw off the habit, Governor O. M. Roberts in later years liked to tell the story of how the two great Texans renewed their friendship just before going to the United States Senate. Desiring to be alone, they climbed atop a 25-foot stack of green lumber in a forest in Shelby County, whittled and toasted their renewed cordiality with frequent pulls from the same bottle and made political plans which resulted in their repeated re-election to the United States Senate.[10]

A ray of sunlight came to the Rusk household at this time with the birth of the first and only daughter, Helena, November 27, 1845. The Rusks had moved to Texas with three children. One child, Thomas J. Rusk, Jr., had died in Georgia. The first one born in Texas was Alonzo, who arrived August 12, 1837, and died in infancy, August 17, 1838. He was followed by Thomas David, April 3, 1841, continuing the first name of his father, but not the middle name.

---

[10]Tolbert, **Day of San Jacinto**.

CHAPTER 24

Among Giants in United States Senate

As always, the interlude with family and friends in the old hometown was far too brief. The turbulent career of the Republic having been brought to a desirable conclusion, General Rusk was called for service in strange new fields. In the campaign for the election of members of the First Texas State Legislature, stress was placed on the fact that the members of that body would have the responsibility of electing two senators for the United States Congress.

Several able men aspired for the honor, but when the Legislature assembled, there was little doubt as to who would be elected. In the joint session of House and Senate February 21, 1846, Rusk and Houston were readily chosen. Rusk received 70 votes, Houston 69 and there were eight scattered votes.

Speaking of Rusk and Houston, John S. Ford remarked that "Texas had two friends to whom she could lean with equal trust and confidence. The impression of the large majority of the people of Texas was that these two great men placed country above self."

Pleased with the honor Texas had bestowed upon him, but not happy over another separation from home, Rusk departed early in March for Washington, D. C. Traveling by what was known as the "eastern route," he reached the capital city March 25 "after a very fatiguing trip" but "enjoyed good health all the way." He took up residence at the National Hotel. Next day, he was introduced in the Senate by Senator Chalmers, was administered the oath, and took his seat.

"I have been cordially received by all parties," he wrote David the following day. "Houston has not yet arrived. . . . I have not yet seen the President but will go up this evening . . . shall be very busy for several days in getting the hang of business here."[1]

---

[1]Rusk Papers, Thos. J. to David Rusk, March 27, 1846.

Houston traveled to Washington by a different route, going by Galveston, New Orleans and St. Louis. He reached Washington in time to call on President Polk Sunday, March 29, and on Monday morning was presented in the Senate by none other than Senator Rusk. To comply with the rule that one-third of the Senate must retire every two years, lots were drawn to determine the tenure of the two Texas Senators. Rusk drew the long term, to expire in 1851, and Houston the short term, ending in 1847. In the House of Representatives, Texas had two members, Timothy Pillsbury and David S. Kaufman.

It took Senator Rusk more than the several days he had mentioned to "get the hang of business." The United States Senate, even in those days, was a unique institution with rules, customs, dignities and trivialities all its own. Texas was the 28th state to enter the Union, and the arrival of the two Texans increased the Senate membership to 56.

Rusk found himself among giants, some friendly, some courteous and some ready to taunt him, but he was not one to be awed by the great men of the age. There was his old friend, John C. Calhoun, the great Southern leader from South Carolina to welcome him. Calhoun was now growing old in years and in service to his country. "He was tall, gaunt and emaciated and had a great mass of hair, angular, somewhat harsh features, and brilliant dark blue eyes."[2] He had just returned to the Senate after a term as Secretary of State.

Calhoun was on the Democratic side of the aisle, and an antagonist on the Whig side was Daniel Webster "with massive overhanging forehead and great speculative eyes," finely dressed and looking the epitome of wisdom.[3] Rusk would later cross him in debate. There was Thomas H. Benton of Missouri, Lewis Cass of Michigan and, presiding over the Senate, was Vice President George Mifflin Dallas. Henry Clay, the "great compromiser," was soon to return to the Senate from Kentucky and play a powerful role. Next year, Abraham Lincoln would take a seat in the House of Representatives and side against Rusk and the Texas delegation on the Mexican War. Ex-President John Quincy Adams was already in the House, fighting every move that might extend slavery. The

---

[2]Wisehart, p. 496.
[3]**Ibid.**

following year, Stephen A. Douglas came to the Senate from Illinois. Rusk was to outlast most of these distinguished statesmen, but not William H. Seward of New York, his personal friend and political adversary, who came to the Senate in 1849.

The 56 members of the Senate were somewhat cramped in the old Senate Chamber, now known as the old Supreme Court Chamber. The room was heated by four fireplaces and two heating stoves burning hickory wood. "Shivering senators sat with their hats on and occasionally wore blankets pinned at their throats. Favorite attire for the dignified solons included "long skirted coats, watch fobs wih heavy seals and beribboned eyeglasses." Snuff was furnished at public expense from a gold-mounted box on the Vice President's desk. It was said that tobacco juice often trickled onto the red carpet.[4] Senator Rusk inclined to the dignified dress of his colleagues, but Senator Houston stuck to informal and sometimes odd attire.

Rusk was not altogether happy during his first session in Congress. The cold Senate Chamber and the winter climate in Washington caused suffering from his rheumatism. He had another annoying ailment aggravated by sitting through long speeches. In fact, his health in general at that time was poor. He found the glamor of service in the august body not all that it had been reputed.

"Think I shall resign when I get home," he wrote his brother, David, June 15, 1846, after less than three months in Washington. Even in the heat of July he wrote, "This is a wretched climate for rheumatism."[5] Possibly he was getting homesick for Texas.

Besides, his political position in the Congress was not a happy one. It was a time when the nation and the Government were torn with strife over the slavery question. Every issue that arose involved the struggle between north and south, slavery and anti-slavery. It had been the great issue for ten years over the annexation of Texas which added to slaveholding territory and which was finally achieved only through jealousy that England might get a foothold in Texas.

Now the first important matter in which Rusk became in-

---

[4]Ibid., pp. 496-97.
[5]Rusk Papers, Thos. J. to David, June 15 and July 8, 1846.

volved in the Senate was the War with Mexico, which began within six weeks of his arrival in Washington. Possibly, the war could have been avoided had President Polk shown more patience and diplomacy. It was a conflict not pleasing to Rusk but one which he was forced by circumstances to defend. The President offered a commission as Major General to Rusk as well as to Sam Houston, but both declined. Rusk, the General, who had so often during the days of the Republic favored aggressive war against Mexico, seemed now to have softened his heart.

Senator Rusk was described as the "working member" of the Texas delegation in the Senate. Senator Houston was not in his glory. "After Texas, the heavy decorum of the Senate was irksome."[6] He soon turned to speech-making over the country and campaigning for the Presidency. The tedious work of assembling facts and figures and presenting speeches in defense of Texas' interests fell largely upon Rusk and he handled the task with great skill and remarkable success. "He knew no fear of opposition, raised by either prejudice or passion," said Senator Seward. "He undertook nothing without first balancing all the chances of success, and gathering in and combing all the available agencies necessary to secure it; and he maintained perfect equanimity until all resistance was overcome."[7]

Rusk soon learned the working of petty politics but failed in his first minor project. David Rusk, sheriff at Nacogdoches, applied for appointment as U. S. marshal for that district and the Senator anticipated no great difficulty in securing the job for him. However, Senator Rusk's friendship with Calhoun proved an obstacle instead of an asset. "I think I am too much suspected of friendship for Calhoun to have as yet much influence with the President", Senator Rusk wrote his brother.[8]

David failed to get the appointment and Thomas J. wrote him: "I have got along very well with the Senate . . . but with the President it is different. I think I was set down at first as being friendly with Calhoun and the consequence is that I have been unable to procure from him a single appointment. He is a weak and vacillating man and is getting very unpopular

[6]Raven, p. 364.
[7]Congressional Globe (Washington, D. C.) Jan. 19, 1858, p. 332.
[8]Rusk Papers, Thos. J. to David, Apr. 18, 1846.

with his own party."[9] Not even Senator Houston backed David Rusk for marshal, being committed to someone else. He was antagonistic to Calhoun over some disagreement of years past.

Rusk had the support of Calhoun on his bill to take the officers and equipment of the Texas navy into the U. S. Navy and another to improve the mail service in Texas. Beyond that, the two friends usually found themselves on opposite sides of national issues such as the Mexican War, the Texas boundary dispute and Calhoun's "Southern Address."[10] It was not long before they clashed in Senate debate: "I had a bout the other day with Mr. Calhoun. Benton swears I beat him badly. At any rate, I carried my point. We had two short speeches apiece."[11]

On the bitter question of slavery, "Rusk steadfastly adhered to the principle of non-interference. He wished neither to enforce nor to restrict slavery, but always threw his weight towards keeping the vexed question in abeyance."[12] Sometimes he exerted his influence in calming bitter controversy and urging fairness on both sides of a question. He chided members on dilatory tactics, the bane of the Senate. "It is my opinion that if we dispose of some business we shall probably get into the habit of doing something," he said on one occasion.[13]

Rusk was soon appointed chairman of the committee on Post Offices and Post Roads. In this capacity, he secured the passage of several bills for the improvement of transportation facilities and mail service. Postmaster General Collamer said Rusk cooperated with him, not from mere duty, but cheerfully and without partisanship. He regarded Rusk as "a man of great clearness of apprehension, soundness of judgment and inflexible integrity of purpose." By clear, frank and forthright arguments, he said, Rusk "secured not only the confidence he desired but the admiration he never sought. It was voluntarily accorded as due to an able and honest man."[14] Collamer was later associated with Rusk as a Senator from Vermont.

From opposite poles politically and geographically, Sena-

---

[9]Ibid., Apr. 28, 1846.
[10]Blount, p. 200.
[11]Rusk Papers, Thos. J. to David, May, 1, 1848
[12]Blount, p. 201.
[13]Stayton, pp. 21, 22.
[14]Congressional Globe, Jan. 19, 1858, p. 332.

tor Seward of New York and Senator Rusk of Texas enjoyed a warm personal friendship. Men of kindred spirit and sensitivity, they could work and dream together. Their service on the Post Office and Post Roads Committee dealt with fortifications, improvements of roads, river and lake navigation within the nation and with sea routes and telegraph communications throughout the world.

"Each of us deplored his ignorance of the regions concerning which we were legislating," said Seward. ". . . we spoke (half seriously and half imaginatively) of going together . . . in a voyage around the world . . . and though it might never be executed, it was still pleasant to contemplate."[15] The sentimental journey never came off.

Between Rusk and Daniel Webster, there was mutual respect. It was said that Webster considered Rusk as first of the young statesman of the South. "The kindest intercourse existed for many years . . . between him and the great Webster," said Senator Gwin of California. "It was rarely they ever opposed each other, except in measures of the strictest party character, where they separated upon a difference of opinion as to great principles. . . . They were men eminently fitted to keep this great Union together, and to stand forth, in this respect, as an example to the living and to posterity."[16] Neither lived to see the great country torn asunder in the Civil War.

---

[15]Ibid., p. 333.
[16]Ibid., p. 332.

CHAPTER 25

Speech Draws National Acclaim

Despite Rusk's thought of resigning at the end of his first session in the Senate, he was back in Washington for the second session of the 29th Congress in December. He had resigned from several public positions during the era of the Republic and had been accused by political opponents of being unstable. If that criticism had been justified at the time it was no longer valid. Now, at 43, he was mature and steadfast. He had entered upon a career that fitted his talents and was to provide some of the most fruitful years of his life.

During the Christmas recess (1846), the entire Texas delegation in Congress, four in number, made a jaunt to New York City. Senators Rusk and Houston and Congressmen Pillsbury and Kaufman were joined by Rusk's oldest son, Benjamin, 18, who had accompanied his father on the return to Washington. "Ben is highly pleased,"[1] Rusk wrote from Baltimore, en route, December 27. The Senator's health was better and he regularly mentioned in his letters for the next few years that his health was good.

The War with Mexico was a source of much controversy and sometimes bitter factionalism during its progress from 1846 to 1848. It was not a "Texas war" as some would have made it. The United States Government had solicited the annexation and approved the compact in spite of Mexico's warning that such action would be interpreted as a declaration of war. Mexico backed her threat by sending troops into what became the disputed territory between the Rio Grande and the Nueces. Gen. Zachary Taylor, with U. S. Troops, drove them out, and the United States declared war May 12, 1846.

The fact that both Texas senators declined commissions of major general, offered them by President Polk, might have indicated their lack of enthusiasm for the conflict. The un-

[1]Rusk Papers, Thos. J. to David, Dec. 27, 1846.

popularity of the Mexican War had a strange parallel in recent times in the Viet Nam War. President Polk was accused of provoking an incident to bring on the war. It was pursued through a series of escalations, with efforts at negotiations failing at each stage. Senator Rusk warned that division of public opinion at home encouraged the Mexicans to continue the fight and prolonged the conflict. He favored vigorous action to bring the war to a conclusion as best for this country as well as for Mexico.

Rusk's opinions were expressed in a set speech in the Senate February 17, 1848. In spite of his snubbing by President Polk when he first came to the Senate, the Texas Senator now found it necessary to defend the President's course in the war. At the same time, he laid the groundwork for a later defense of Texas' claim to the territory beyond the Nueces River, as well as the New Mexico area east of the Rio Grande.

Rusk's familiarity with every event in the history of the Texas Republic served him well in presenting proof that the area between the Nueces and the Rio Grande was legally American soil, secured by Texas treaties with Santa Anna. The Mexicans had retired beyond the Rio Grande in 1836, he pointed out, adding that "They had never since supposed that they had any claim on that east side. . . . The Texans took possession of the territory, and had kept possession of it ever since. It was occupied chiefly by the widows of those who had fallen in the contest with Santa Anna. . . . Texas could never be induced to withdraw protection from these widows and their orphans."[2]

The speech was in effect an answer to the accusations of such leading Whigs as Clay and Webster in the Senate and Abraham Lincoln in the House, that the war was "wantonly started to despoil a weaker nation and to obtain . . . territory for the expansion of Southern interest." Abraham Lincoln had introduced in the House the so-called "Spot Resolution," requiring the President to locate the spot where American blood had been shed, and to inform the House whether the "citizens" referred to in his message had not been armed

---

[2]**Congressional Globe,** 30th Congress, Feb., 17, 1848, Summary of Rusk's speech on Mexican war, p. 375.

soldiers,[3] an insinuation that the incident had been provoked to start the war.

In his address, Rusk referred to outrages committed by Mexicans in the area and cited the attack on a family of 16 persons, "two of them ladies, the latter of whom were outraged, and the whole afterwards murdered, and the fingers of these ladies were cut off, and carried into Mexico as trophies. He asserted that if the dungeons of Mexico could have been searched, there would have been no two years when some American citizens would not have been found incarcerated, without any charge against them."[4]

He declared the President had made so many attempts during the course of the war to negotiate "as almost to subject himself to ridicule." He urged vigorous prosecution of the war to show Mexico we are determined "to force a peace out of her."[5] It so happened that in far-away Mexico, General Winfield Scott was doing just that. The Treaty of Guadalupe Hidalgo had been signed February 2 and it was ratified by the Senate March 10. Mexico relinquished all claims to Texas, including that beyond the Nueces, and ceded that part of the present United States west of Texas and of the Louisiana Purchase, and south of Oregon, which included New Mexico and California. The United States paid Mexico $15,000,000 and assumed the claims of American citizens against that country.

Texas had supported the War with heavy enlistments of volunteers who fought bravely and well. However, there were some who were accused by Gen. Zachary Taylor of atrocities against Mexican civilians. In letters from Army Headquarters at Monterrey to the Adjutant General of the Army on October 6, 1846, and June 16, 1847, General Taylor complained of the conduct of Texas mounted volunteers and requested that "no more troops may be sent to this column from the State of Texas."[6] During the presidential campaign of 1848, when Taylor was running on the Whig ticket, these letters became a subject of controversy, and Senator Rusk came to the defense of conduct of Texas soldiers in the War. Taylor denied having written the slanderous letters.

---

[3]Spillman, W. J., **Adjustment of the Texas Boundary in 1860, Texas State Historical Association Quarterly,** VII, p. 161.
[4]**Congressional Globe,** Feb. 17, 1848, p. 375.
[5]**Ibid.**
[6]Rusk Papers, copies of Taylor letters to Adjutant General.

"Genl. Taylor has . . . placed himself in this as he has done on several other questions, in a condition to be quoted upon both sides," Rusk wrote the editor of the *Galveston News*. "Where it is popular to abuse Texas, his two letters to the Adjutant General furnish ample material. Where it is otherwise, the remark attributed to him at Buena Vista, 'That he would give his plantation on the Mississippi River for one hour of Hays' Texas Rangers,' must answer the purpose."[7]

Rusk's speech on the Mexican War in February, 1848, drew wide attention over the nation. As usual, he confided his private feelings to his brother, David; this time he was almost jubilant: "I have made a speech in Congress which has given me a very good stand and I think it is the part of prudence now to be modest and as far as possible unassuming. If I can just manage to hold the position I now occupy it is sufficiently prominent to satisfy my ambition. Kaufman and Houston are both anxious to make speeches but are a little doubtful.

"My speech had a great run. It has been called for all over the country and upwards of a hundred thousand have been printed and circulated, besides having been printed in most of the Democratic papers. I know you will be pleased at my success but for fear you will get tired of my bragging, I will just drop the subject."

Rusk's letter was written from New York, May 7, 1848. "I had labored hard at Washington all winter and felt quite exhausted and tired and a week ago came to the conclusion that I would come off here rest and recruit a few days. I have been the working member of the delegation this Session. Houston has been traveling about, electioneering for the nomination for the Presidency. He is so anxious for it that he is almost crazy but I fear he won't get it."

Concerning Texas Congressman Pillsbury, Rusk added a remark intended only for eyes of a trusted brother: "Pillsbury has divided his time between drinking and getting married. His wife is a little old but a woman of very good sense." As to Congressman Kaufman, he was appointed on the committee to bury Rep. John Quincy Adams, who had died recently. On his tour, Kaufman made "one or two speeches which has had the effect to swell him up considerably. Kaufman, bar-

---

[7]Rusk Papers, Rusk to Editor of **Galveston News.**

ring his selfishness, is a pretty good fellow and is very friendly to you."

With his growing prestige, Rusk was receiving invitations to speak in various places but thought it wise to decline. "I was invited yesterday to go on board of a British steamer and make a speech, but I think I acted prudently by declining," he mentioned in his letter to David from New York.[8]

It was Presidential election year, and Senator Rusk found that in New York as well as in Washington the all absorbing subject was the Presidency. In his opinion, the Whigs as well as his own Democratic party were bad off for material. "I fear whichever party may succeed, we will have a jackass in the chair," he lamented.[9] Rusk was actively helping Houston in his campaign and felt that it would be good for Texas if he could be elected, but was not hopeful. He assisted Charles Edward Lester in writing the book, *Sam Houston and His Republic,* intended to advance Houston's candidacy. In the end Houston did not allow his name to go before the Convention.

---

[8]Rusk Papers, Thos. J. to David, from New York, May 7, 1848.
[9]**Ibid.**

CHAPTER 26

The Better Years

Congenial family life contributed to Rusk's success as well as his peace of mind. Unselfish Mary Rusk never resented being left alone with the burden of family responsibilities. Rather, she did everything possible to encourage her husband in his career and rejoiced with him at his growing success and the honors bestowed upon him. The two older sons were growing into manhood and were a source of pride.

The eldest, Benjamin Livingston, called Ben, accompanied his father to Washington for the opening of Congress in December, 1846. The second son, John, aspired to follow in his father's profession as a lawyer. Rusk wrote his father-in-law, Gen. Benjamin Cleveland, with fatherly pride:

> "Benjamin is very study [sic] and industrious and is more inclined to the farm than anything else and it is a principle with me to give a child a fair opportunity to follow the bent of his mind if it takes an honorable direction. He is very active, stout and healthy and gives earnest of making a man of energy. John wishes to become a lawyer and I intend, if I live, to give him a fair chance. He is well behaved and has, if I am not greatly mistaken, talent sufficient to succeed. Cicero and Tom are both pert boys and the daughter [Helena] is one of the finest children I have ever seen of her age. But Polly will, as a mother of course, boast of her to you."[1]

The following year, Rusk wrote, "Ben, I think, is inclined to be industrious and careful and if he will steer of frolicking and bad company, I think will succeed."[2] There was a question in February, 1848, when John was 20 as to whether he should continue in the local school at Nacogdoches. The matter was discussed in a rare letter of Mrs. Rusk's. Though she wrote often to her husband, very few of her quaint writings

---

[1]Rusk Papers, Rusk to Benjamin Cleveland, Dec. 18, 1847.
[2]Ibid., Thos. J. to David Rusk, May 7, 1848.

have been preserved. Just as her husband never found a need for punctuation marks, Mrs. Rusk was never hampered by spelling and got over her message quite clearly. To Rusk in Washington she wrote:

> "the school is jauste oute and the trustees have ritten on for more teachers, a gentleman and his wife and daughter from new orleans. they are expected soon to take charge of the school. I want you to write me whether you think ite is beste for benjamin to gow the nexte session or note if he is wiling to doo sow. I thinke ite would be the beste for him if hee is wiling to doo sow but if he is note, ite will note bee worth while to sende him. I will talke with him on the subjecte and write you . . ."[3]

The author has found no record as to whether Benjamin remained in school. The second son, John Cleveland, was with Senator Rusk in Washington at that time. Mrs. Rusk's letter continued:

> you must write me whate you thinke of John, whether you thinke he will be ruddy or note or whether he shows any disposition to be wilede, and if he dose doo, for lordes sake check him in begining, tell him ite is the wish and sinsear prair of his mother thate hee may pursue a ruddy corse which will make both his parence and himself happy. . . . you now thate hee is a strange disposition and wee must doo the way thate wee thinke will do the beste for him."[4]

John, then 18, was in Washington filling a clerkship in the Navy Department, with a salary of $75 a month. "He likes to go to the theater but is very punctual and attentive to his business," his father wrote.[5] He was of a more scholarly turn than his older brother and received some college training. While working in Washington, he studied law on the side, as his father had done back in South Carolina, and was admitted to the bar in Nacogdoches when he was 21. In later years, he served as administrator of the Thomas J. Rusk estate.[6]

As the session of Congress in 1848 continued beyond the Fourth of July and Washington weather waxed hot and humid,

---

[3]**Ibid.**, Mary Rusk to Husband, Feb. 21, 1848.
[4]**Ibid.**
[5]Rusk Papers, Thos. J. to David Rusk, March 25, 1848.
[6]Probate Court Records, County Clerk's Office, Nacogdoches.

the Senator's dreams turned wistfully toward home. "My Dear Mary: I shall be half crazy from this time until I get home. My anxiety always increases as the time draws nearer. . . . I would write more but I am pressed and am bothered with a bad pen and greasy ink."[7]

The resentment which Mrs. Rusk's parents had felt against Son-in-Law Rusk after his debacle in Georgia which resulted in his removal to Texas was soon healed. General and Mrs. Cleveland were proud of his success. General Cleveland wrote often to Rusk, usually addressing him as "Dear General" and occasionally as "Dear Tom." He was a dyed-in-the-wool Southerner and freely expressed his opinions in friendly fashion to Senator Rusk, who was not always of the same mind. At one time he visited Texas and through some transaction acquired some land, which he decided to will to his Texas grandchildren, the heirs of Ann Thorn and Mary Rusk. The rest of the estate, after the deaths of General and Mrs. Cleveland, was to be divided between the three daughters, the third daughter being Catherine Hoyle.[8]

These were among the better years for Thomas J. and Mary Rusk. "Polly's health is greatly improved and in addition to our gradual improvements in the comforts of life and the happiness of seeing her children grow up creditably around her, that well-founded hope which she has of future happiness based upon the truths of Christianity renders her happy and contented," Rusk wrote to Mary's father, and added, "You should write her often. As her age increases, so does her affection increase towards you and her mother."[9]

For his own part, Rusk evidently had been able to conquer his drinking problem. After his over-indulgence in Austin in 1845, there is no record of any other "spree". In the Senate, he, as well as his colleague, Houston, cultivated good company. "I have had the good fortune here to acquire the friendship of very many of those whose good opinion is more desirable, as well amongst Whigs as Democrats," he reported with some pride to his father-in-law. "My health is much better than it has been for years past, which I attribute in a great measure under Providence to the change in my habits."[10]

---

[7]Rusk Papers, Rusk to wife, Mary, July 7, 1848.
[8]Ibid., Rusk to Cleveland, April 13, 1850.
[9]Ibid.
[10]Ibid.

Dreaming of the future, as all men must, Rusk hoped in a few years to relieve himself of "pecuniary embarrassment" and retire from the "turmoil of political life to provide for my children and take care of the comfort of her who has been my surest resource for advice and aid in all the trying moments of my not uneventful life for the past twenty one years."[11]

It had always been Rusk's practice to write regularly to his family while he was away in the public service. He was punctual at writing to his wife and children while in the Senate, as well as to his mother in South Carolina and his in-laws in Georgia. He always confided in his brother, David, and the latter preserved his letters, providing a remarkable source of information. Comparatively few of his letters to his immediate family and other relatives have been preserved.

One letter which Rusk wrote to his 15-year-old son, Cicero, is found among the Rusk papers. It is evidence that the Senator was more particular about spelling than of punctuation. The letter follows, just as written—without a single punctuation mark:

"Washington 14th Feby 1850
"My Dear Son
    "I have just received your letter of the 17th Jany last I am delighted with the improvement which you have made in writing and have only to request you to pay attention to your spelling now is the time to learn how to spell and write well I am very glad to hear that you are all well I wish you to write me often I am very well
        "Your affectionate father
        "Tho J Rusk
"Mr. Cicero Rusk"[12]

---

[11]**Ibid.**
[12]Rusk Papers, Thos. J. to Cicero Rusk, Feb. 14, 1850.

CHAPTER 27

"The First and Last Drop of Blood"

"Sir, I believe that the State which I in part represent, if certain destruction stared her in the face, would assert her rights; and in their maintenance here she is entitled to my best exertions. I have served her in youth, she has honored me in age, and she is entitled to the first and the last drop of blood that runs in my veins in the defense of her just and constitutional rights, against all opposition, however formidable.

"Now, how stands this question and upon whom does the responsibility of drawing the sword fall? Or has it indeed come to this, that, because the Government of the United States is a powerful one, it alone can draw and flourish the sword, while everybody else must remain quiet, no matter how just and righteous their position may be. . . ."[1]

With grave countenance but subdued voice, Senator Rusk was speaking. Senator Clay listened with deep concern, Senator Webster was in serious thought. The Northern abolitionists sat sternly silent and the Southern senators alone registered approval. The debate on the Compromise Bill of 1850 had dragged on for nearly eight months and now, at the end of the hot summer, nerves were frayed and tempers easily flared. Even the mild-tempered Rusk had flared up once, back in June—now it was late July.

"We are in great excitement upon the compromise," he had written David on June 9. "The Texas part of it has been up for two days. Houston did not take part. I got on extremely well with the exception of losing my temper a little yesterday. The debate will be in the papers, and I will send you copies of it." Several days later, he wrote again to David: "I have just made another speech upon the Texas claim to Santa Fe. It was short but said by good judges to be the best yet made. . . . The prospect for passage of Clay's compromise bill is very fa-

---

[1]Appendix to the **Congressional Globe,** 31st Congress, 1st Session, July 24, 1850, pp. 1421-22.

vorable; if it passes we shall get at least ten million for all the land above El Paso on the Rio Grande."[2]

The matter of slavery had been brought into the debate and became the main issue, a struggle between North and South. With Texas, it was a fight to hold the land for which its patriots had fought and through ten years of adversity under the Republic had maintained. Rusk resented the injection of the slave issue. Texas had entered the Union as a slave state but now the anti-slavery forces sought to trim down her size to create more free soil.

In the debate back during the Mexican War, Rusk had ably defended the claim of Texas and the United States to the area between the Nueces and the Rio Grande. The main issue now was the line of the upper Rio Grande in the Santa Fe region. The western boundary as claimed by the Texas Republic when it was annexed to the Union included half of what is now New Mexico. The crisis of the debate now raging in the Senate arose when a resolution was introduced to fix the western boundary of Texas along the general lines that exist today, by excluding all of New Mexico and the northern strip that reached into Colorado and Wyoming, together with parts of present Oklahoma and Kansas.

Throughout the months of debate, Rusk steadfastly contended for the Rio Grande from its mouth at the Gulf of Mexico to its source in the mountains of Colorado as the western boundary of Texas. He followed his usual systematic method of presenting all the facts and documents, building his case step by step with his complete knowledge of every detail. No other man was so well informed on the matter and none could refute his argumnt. After all, it was Rusk, while still camped on the battlefield of San Jacinto, who had first put in writing the claim of Texas of the Rio Grande as its western boundary. It was included in the penciled memorandum which he handed to President Burnet which formed the basis of the treaty with Santa Anna.

During the current debate in Congress, attempts were made to postpone the decision by several devices, one of which was to take the case to the Supreme Court. Rusk contended, against Clay and others, that the Court had no jurisdiction over the matter. As to Texas and the court action, he warned that

[2]Rusk Papers, Thos. J. to David Rusk, June 9 and 17, 1850.

"you may force it upon her; you may drag her before the Supreme Court; you may wrest the territory from her hands; but in my humble judgment you have no excuse to justify such action, and you will have to do it by power."[3]

Some charged that Texas only recently had laid claim to the area in dispute, a charge which Rusk easily refuted:

"Now, Sir, it is just the reverse; the Government of the United States has *recently advanced* a claim to this territory. Texas has claimed this territory since 1835. After her first victory over her enemy . . . Texas designated the Rio Grande as her boundary. After the capture of Santa Anna . . . she again asserted this boundary. In 1836 she asserted it upon her statue-book, and when the government of the United States made an overture to Texas, repeating it twice, and asked her to become a part and parcel of the union, she was claiming this very boundary."[4]

In an effort at compromise, Senator Clay proposed that the federal government, for the sake of harmony, pay Texas a reasonable sum for the relinquishment of the claim to New Mexico territory. Rusk replied that the title of Texas to all of New Mexico east of the Rio Grande was incontrovertible and protested any attempt to dismember Texas as a peace offering to those who would encroach on her rights.

However, by July, when all efforts at reason had failed and Texas' boundary claims seemed hopeless, being bound up in sectional prejudices, Rusk decided it was best to salvage what was possible by securing the best deal obtainable in payment for the territory which would doubtless be taken by force. This territory, he said, belongs to Texas "by every just title—it is hers now. She owes just debts and she cannot yield without a just compensation." Texas "will insist on those rights as secured to her in the resolutions of annexation, and the treaty which followed them." He appealed to the senators to "meet the question fairly and on its own merits— to avoid mixing it up with the question of slavery or no slavery—and to decide the question on the principles of justice. This is all Texas asks; and this is what she has a right . . . to expect."[5]

---

[3] Appen. to **Congressional Globe**, 31st Cong., 1st Sesn., 1850, p. 923.
[4] Ibid., pp. 1259-60.
[5] Ibid., p. 1260.

The mention of "adequate compensation" brought taunts that Texas was trying "to coin money out of the United States by means of the admiration which she had excited." Here Rusk aimed his darts at his northern friend, Senator Seward of New York. The charge was unkind, he said, "particularly as coming from a Senator some of whose constituents, without ever looking at a map, without ever examing the treaty [of annexation], have been pronouncing judgment against Texas in this controversy, for the purpose of keeping open this interminable agitation of the slave question."

As to the matter of "coining money" out of the United States, he declared that the United States, instead of doing Texas a favor by buying her rightful territory, was due the State compensation for allowing the United States Indians to commit terrible depredations on Texas soil during the time of the Republic, depredations which were continuing even at that very moment.

> "While you are seeking to take our territory from us
> . . . four or five hundred of your Indians, driven out of
> Florida and other states, are upon the soil of Texas, and
> engaged at this moment in hostilities and in depredations
> upon the property and lives of our citizens, without re-
> gards to age, sex, or condition. Such, sir, is the true state
> of the facts, but we have not complained . . . but when
> . . . you ask us to submit to the sword that ought to be
> drawn in our defense, and to march on and off the terri-
> tory as the Executive Government may direct, I hope you
> will not believe that we will tamely submit to such wrong
> and degredation."[6]

While the war of words went on in Congressional halls, the line of battle was being drawn in New Mexico. Governor Peter H. Bell of Texas had dispatched a commissioner with full powers to extend civil jurisdiction over four unorganized counties in the disputed area in New Mexico. But the United States officer serving as military governor of New Mexico, with headquarters at Santa Fe took steps to establish a territorial government which would have included the area claimed by Texas.

Thus the lines were drawn. Governor Bell addressd a letter to President Fillmore, asking whether the action of the

6Ibid., p. 1261.

military governor of New Mexico had the President's approval. With armed conflict threatened between Texas and United States forces, Governor Bell convened the Legislature to deal with the matter and President Fillmore sent an urgent message to Congress asking a prompt settlement of the issue. Senator Clay and other moderates were alarmed and avidly sought a peaceful settlement. Armed conflict on the upper Rio Grande, Mr. Clay believed, would set off a chain reaction resulting in civil war. Senator Winthrop, who by this time had succeeded Webster, said he would rather have the "boundary run by gold rather than steel; by money rather than blood."[7]

It was Senator Pierce of Maryland who offered a bill fixing the boundaries of Texas approximately as they now stand and offering the State $10,000,000 in payment for the vast territory ceded, half of the money to be reserved for the payment of Texas debts filed with the United States.

Senator Houston said he would support the bill, not from pecuniary or sectional interest, but in order to conciliate and reconcile the best interests of the country.

Rusk said he felt certain that if the bill passed with his vote, "I forfeit my seat in this Senate. I shall do it cheerfully. I shall look beyond into a peace and quiet; to a time when affection and good feeling will exist between Texas and the balance of the United States. . . ."[8] He voted for the bill. In the House of Representatives, Texas Congressmen Howard and Kaufman, who had been active in defending the interests of Texas, also supported the bill. It was adopted by both houses of Congress and the offer accepted by the Texas Legislature. For ten million dollars, Texas had given up one-third of the territory within the boundaries of the old Republic.

The Texas Boundary settlement was a key part of the famous Compromise of 1850—the part which had prolonged the debate and on which the whole package agreement hinged. Included in the compromise sponsored by Mr. Clay and finally adopted was the admission of California as a free state, and creation of the territories of New Mexico and Utah without restrictions as to slavery. Clay, in his old age, had won his greatest victory. Senator Rusk, in his prime, had accomplished

[7] Ibid., p. 1560.
[8] Ibid., p. 1577.

a just settlement for Texas. The Civil War had been postponed for a decade.

But the great Southerner, Calhoun, was not there to suffer defeat. He had faced Clay in debate early in the discussion. Seeing the power of the South gradually slipping away, he said to the Northern Senators, "If you who represent the stronger portion cannot agree to settle [the issues involved] on the broad principles of justice and duty, say so; and let the states we represent agree to separate and part in peace."[9]

Calhoun had tottered into the Senate Chamber from a sick bed and was so infirm that he sat and listened while his speech was read by a friend. It was his last appearance in the Senate, and before he left the chamber on that occasion, he had a friendly chat with his former law student, Thomas J. Rusk. That was on February 5; two months later, he died.

"Mr. Calhoun is dead," Rusk wrote to his brother on April 2. "He died last Sunday morning. Yesterday his death was announced in both branches of Congress. I felt it due to Texas, myself and the occasion to say a few words. . . . I feel gratified after our difference of opinion last winter and the efforts which had been made by some in Texas to make us enemies that we remained friends until his last hour. The last conversation which he held in the Senate Chamber was with me and of a most friendly character. The funeral took place today and there was an immense concourse of people."[10]

In his address to the Senate, Rusk said of his old friend, ". . . it will be a source of pleasant, though sad reflection to me through life, to remember, that on the last day on which he occupied his seat in this chamber, his body worn by disease, but his mind as vigorous as ever, we held a somewhat extended conversation on the exciting topics of the day, in which the same kind feeling which had so strongly impressed me in youth, were still manifested toward me by the veteran statesman."[11]

Rusk was joined by Daniel Webster, often an opponent of Calhoun on great national issues, in eulogizing the great Southerner. Senator Andrew P. Butler, Calhoun's colleague from

[9]Bassett, John Spencer, **A Short History of the United States,** (The Macmillan Co., New York, 1914) p. 456.
[10]Rusk Papers, Thos. J. to David Rusk, April 2, 1850.
[11]**Abridgement of Debates of Congress, 1846-1850,** XVI, pp. 473-74.

South Carolina, also delivered a warm tribute to the able defender of the rights of the South.

To some degree, the mantle of Calhoun fell to Jefferson Davis, Senator from Mississippi, who later became President of the Confederacy.

CHAPTER 28

Proposed for President

The year 1850 had been a successful one for Thomas J. Rusk. His long battle in the Senate for the rights of Texas had been exhausting at times, requiring work day and night, as the burden of the debate fell to his lot. He had the satisfaction of knowing that he had obtained the best settlement possible on the boundary dispute. After all was said and done, it was a healthy arrangement for Texas. Even had she been able to retain all of her territory, it doubtless would have been divided later into several states.

Furthermore, the ten million dollars to settle her burdensome debts placed the state in position to develop her resources, and relinquishing the vast, remote areas relieved her of the burden of attempting to govern and police the wild lands. Texas was now in a position to grow and prosper after 15 years of struggle for survival.

Rusk's concern as to whether the settlement would be acceptable to the people back home was not without basis. The plan was rejected in a popular election. However, the Legislature accepted the deal anyway. Instead of losing his seat as he had predicted, the Legislature re-elected him for another six-year term.

"The acceptance of the Ten Millions by Texas has gratified a large majority of both parties [in Congress] and Texas as a State stands better now than she has ever done before," Rusk wrote his brother following his return to Washington in January, 1851, after spending the time between sessions at home. "I think the prospect good to pass a law to raise two additional Regiments of Cavalry for the defense of our frontier. Kaufman and Howard [Representatives] are both here with their families and well. Genl. Houston has not arrived nor have I heard a word from him. A good many are talking about running him for President." Rusk grumbled a little: "Texas has only one senator. All the work falls on me."[1]

---

[1] Rusk Papers, Thos J. to David Rusk, Jan. 6, 1851.

148

Besides his work on the floor of the Senate during the past year, Rusk carried a heavy load of committee assignments. He served on five committees. Between debates on the floor, he had prepared an extensive report from his committee on Post Offices and Post Roads on the subject of reducing postal rates and repealing franking privileges. The report had required "a great deal of labor."[2]

Altogether, it was a time of fulfillment and an unusual degree of tranquility for Rusk. His work in the Senate was challenging and gratifying. His health was the best it had been for a number of years. After fifteen years, he was recovering financially and spiritually from the disaster which had overtaken him as a young lawyer in Georgia in 1835. He had said some time ago that he never expected to be rich "but I begin to look forward to the day when I shall get clear of my embarrassment and be comfortably off."[3]

The ability which Rusk had demonstrated in handling the Texas Boundary question and in supporting the Compromise of 1850 added to his prestige in the Senate and brought him a degree of national prominence. He was widely mentioned for the Democratic nomination for President. By May, 1852, as the time of the party convention at Baltimore was drawing near, letters were sent out to several leading Democrats who had been mentioned for the presidency, Rusk among them. "I answered promptly and fully and declared myself not a candidate," Rusk wrote.

But Houston, along with Cass, Douglas, Buchanan and Marcy were contending for the nomination. Rusk described Houston as "remarkably anxious" and a little jealous of him (Rusk). "It will nearly kill him if he fails. I mean in good faith and sincerity to press his claims. I think he would be better than any other candidate and I am sure it would be better for Texas that he should be President."[4]

During the convention, Rusk's supporters continued to urge him to allow his name to be presented, either for President or Vice President, but he steadfastly declined. Nevertheless, he was pleased at the esteem in which he was held. "You would be a little astonished at the number and respectability of the men who wish to nominate me but I will not permit myself

---

[2]Ibid. June 17, 1850.
[3]Ibid., May 7, 1848.
[4]Ibid., May 19, 1852.

to think of such a thing," he confided in a letter to Brother David.[5] Both Rusk and Houston were delegates at the week-long convention in which a dark horse, Franklin Pierce of New Hampshire, was nominated on the 49th ballot and went on to be elected President. In the deadlocked convention, Rusk might have had as good chance as anyone for the honor.

Ever watchful for the interests of Texas, Senator Rusk was careful to see that the provisions of the Boundary Settlement and the debt payment were carried out. In 1852 he disclosed a discrepancy in the boundary survey that would have cost Texas 3,400 square miles of territory. His revelation brought repercussions all the way to the White House, then occupied by Whig President Millard Fillmore.

"I made a decided hit the other day in the Senate which has caused some trouble in high quarters," Rusk wrote to his brother. "The Commissioner to run the boundary with Mexico gave away in violation of the Treaty a slip of territory above El Paso of thirty-four by one hundred miles. The surveyor protested against it. The Secretary of Interior and the President approved the conduct of the Commissioner. Last week a bill came up to appropriate money for the survey. I offered and carried an amendment repudiating the conduct of the Commissioner, thus rebuking the President and Secretary. This matter will doubtless kick up a row but I am well posted up and on the right side and fully ready for it."[6]

Under the Boundary Settlement in 1850, the Federal Government retained half of the ten million dollars in the treasury for payment of the Texas debts. The five million in U. S. bonds which was paid to the State of Texas was used to pay the State's operating expenses, thus making it possible to relinquish all the State tax revenues to the counties and schools. One-tenth of the revenue went to the school fund and the other nine-tenths to the counties to enable them to build courthouses and jails and to serve other needs.

In the meantime, little was done by either State or Federal Government toward actually paying the debts owed by the Republic at the time Texas became a state. Texas now placed additional claims against the Federal Government specifically for

---

[5]Ibid.
[6]Ibid. May 24, 1852.

debts incurred by the old Republic in defending its frontiers against Indians from the United States.

Senator Rusk pressed the whole matter of settlement of debts in a speech in the Senate July 19, 1854, which led to final adjustment of the pressing matter. He reminded the Senate that the creditors' claims that had been presented under the Compromise of 1850 had been referred to the Committee on Finance and delayed there until it was too late in each session of Congress to act on the matter.

At the same time, the Senator from Texas pointed out that "a very large portion of that debt had been created by the necessity of defending ourselves against the Indians of the United States, whom this government was bound by every principle of humanity and good neighborhood, as well as by treaty obligations, to restrain, but utterly failed to do so. By this failure . . . they subjected Texas, at vast expense of blood and treasure, to defend herself . . ."[7]

Rusk proceeded to show that the United States was obligated under its treaty with Mexico in 1828, prior to Texas independence, to control the Indians and that this responsibility continued binding with reference to the Texas Republic. He then presented an itemized statemnt by Texas Comptroller James B. Shaw, of expenses incurred by the Republic in "maintaining peace with and protecting her frontiers from the incursions of Indians removed thither and belonging to the United States." The total was $3,815,011.01. "I believe this claim to be just. . . . I shall, . . . as long as Texas honors me . . . as her representative, continue to press this claim until it shall be paid."[8]

Congress passed a bill in February, adding $2,750,000 to the $5,000,000 already provided, to be distributed pro rata among the creditors. Furthermore, Texas was refunded $299,602 which she already had paid on the debt. Settlement of these claims improved still further Texas' excellent financial condition. Rusk had led the fight for the ten million in 1850 and added his strength to this final settlement in 1855. In such sound financial status, the State proceeded to a great era of economic growth and development.

However, there was some opposition back home to accepting the settlement, generous though it seems from an impartial

---

[7]Rusk's Speech on **The Texas Debt,** delivered in the Senate July 19, 1854, leaflet in Texas State Library.
[8]**Ibid.**

point of view. "I cannot think there is anything derogatory to Texas in the bill, Rusk wrote the editor of the *Austin State Gazette*. He added:

> "The difference of what Texas would receive in money if the debt were settled under the provisions of our [Texas] law, over what she would receive if the act of Congress be accepted, would, I suppose be about six hundred thousand dollars. Is that sum worth a ten years' controversy, with but a slender prospect of obtaining it in the end. I think not. . . . My anxiety to see the state out of debt, the high estimate which I place on such a state of affairs in promoting the future prosperity of the state, may possibly have misled my judgement."[9]

*   *   *

Just as Rusk and Houston had differed in the days of the Republic over the Indian question, they were now on opposite sides of the slavery issue which was splitting the nation apart. They had acted together in refusing to sign Calhoun's Southern Address or to attend his caucus of Southern Congressmen which they feared was a step toward dismemberment of the Union. It was an easy decision for Houston, who hated Calhoun, but more difficult for Rusk, a personal friend and beneficiary of the great Southern leader. Here Rusk's moral courage to stand for what he considered right, regardless of personal friendship, had been tested. Now it was to be put to the test again as he found it necessary to differ with his friend and colleague, Sam Houston.

The slavery question erupted again when legislation was introduced to organize the Kansas and Nebraska territories. After a bitter debate, an amendment by Senator Douglas to allow the people of the territories to decide for themselves whether they should be slave or free was adopted. It was the principle of non-intervention which had been applied in 1850 in the cases of New Mexico and Utah. Consistent with his previous policy, Rusk voted for the Kansas-Nebraska Bill, believing the people of the states which would eventually be created should have the right to decide their own affairs.

Both Douglas and Houston were ambitious for the presi-

---

[9] Austin State Gazette, May 12, 1855.

dential chair. Each was playing for support of both North and South but took opposite tacks. Houston voted against the Kansas-Nebraska measure which Douglas supported. Neither gained very much politically from his action. Each failed in his bid for the presidency.

CHAPTER 29

Against the "Know-Nothings"

Rusk strongly opposed the "Know-Nothing" Party which emerged in the early 1850's and flourished for a few years. This secret political society favored harsh restrictions on Roman Catholics and naturalized aliens. The "Know-Northings" acquired considerable strength in Texas as well as in other states, both north and south. In fact, the new party succeeded in electing Nathaniel P. Banks of Massachusetts as Speaker of the House of Representatives in 1856. Rusk was outraged; he wrote David:

> "Yesterday the House elected Banks, an abolition Know Nothing speaker by three votes over Gov. Aiken of South Carolina. Not a single Know Nothing from a non-slave holding state voting for Aiken and about eighty of them voting for Banks. So much for the mongrel party. The Southern man who is deceived by them hereafter will be so because he wants to be deceived."[1]

Rusk objected bitterly to the secrecy of the organization. How could an American surrender his judgment to "a midnight council and bind himself by an oath to carry out what they dictate, and fulfill his obligation to himself, his country and his God as a freeman?" He said the party was out purely for office and power.[2]

Strangely enough, Sam Houston supported the Know-Nothing movement, though its doctrines seemed antithetic to his whole nature and political philosophy. He brought the issue home to Texas. Like a bolt from the blue came a letter to Rusk from Houston, dated Huntsville, May 12, 1857:

> "Today I have declared myself a candidate for Governor, and will as soon as I can visit your town. You will be surprised . . . for you know it was my intention to retire

---

[1]Rusk papers, Thos J. to David Rusk, Jan. 3, 1856.
[2]Stayton, p. 25.

from the Senate to private life. They marked the space, as they declared 'Houston and anti Houston.' So now the whips crack & the longest pole will bring down the persimmons.

"The people want excitement and I had as well give it as any one."[3]

The whips cracked mightily as always in Houston's political campaigns but his pole was not long enough to "bring down the persimmons." He was roundly defeated by Hardin R. Runnels, but kept his seat in the Senate. Rusk refused to be drawn directly into the campaign. There were several friendly letters from Houston, one on May 28 as he was preparing to speak in Nacogdoches: "Dear Genl., I will be happy to see you, before I speak, I only wish 10 or 15 minutes talk. The stage waits. On Saturday in your town at 2 Oclk P.M. Thine Truly, Houston."[4]

Friendly personal relations were maintained but Rusk could not stomach the Know-Nothing policies. A letter which he had written two years before was used to indicate that he was opposed to Houston's candidacy. Addressed to M. D. Ector, it had been published in the Galveston News, July 24, 1855: "No party can be safely trusted with power who does not openly avow their principles. The oaths which it is understood they take are illegal, tyrannical, and at open war with the fundamental principles of our Government. . . . At the north, as all the elections show, they are abolitionists. At the south they profess to be pro-slavery men."[5]

Two years later, Houston ran again for Governor and defeated Runnels, but Rusk had not lived to see this development.

While Rusk was gaining stature and influence in Congress, he maintained his popularity in Texas. In fact, there was never a time throughout his career from 1835 until his death in 1857 that his favor with the people was seriously impaired. His support of the Kansas-Nebraska bill and Houston's opposite view had some repercussions in Texas and the matter came up in the State Legislature. A joint resolution was introduced instructing both Texas Senators to vote against repeal or modification of the Kansas-Nebraska bill. A substitute was offered by Representative F. M. White of Port Lavaca, commending the course of Senator Rusk on the Kansas-Nebraska act and making

[3]Rusk Papers, Houston to Rusk from Huntsville, May 12, 1857.
[4]Ibid., from Alto, May 28, 1857.
[5]Galveston News, July 24, 1855.

no mention of Senator Houston. This brought on much discussion and no action was taken at that time.

However, the Legislature met in joint session and expressed its approval of Rusk's service by re-electing him by unanimous vote for another six-year term, though his current term would not expire for another full year. This was on November 15, 1855. Two weeks later, the Legislature passed a resolution approving "the course of Thomas J. Rusk, in voting for the Kansas-Nebraska Act," and disapproving the "course of Sam Houston in voting against it." The vote was 73 to 3.[6]

Though Rusk was involved in the monumental issues of the Nation, he never neglected the lesser matters affecting the welfare of Texas. He secured an appropriation of $100,000 for the exploration of artesian wells for the western plains of Texas as a source of water for travelers and livestock passing over that route to California and Mexico. He worked to secure a wagon road from El Paso westward to California. During his service in Congress he was able to secure vast improvements in mail lines and mail stages in Texas. He was instrumental in legislation giving relief to veterans of the Texas Navy during the Republic.[7]

One of the greater projects on which Rusk exerted a continuing effort through many years was the proposed transcontinental railroad. The dream of ribbons of steel stretching from the Mississippi across Texas to California was not realized until 24 years after his death, but he is due credit for promoting the idea and laying the groundwork. It would have been realized years earlier had not the Civil War intervened.

In September, 1853, he accompanied a party on a long trek across Texas, scouting out the route and promoting interest in the proposed railway. Most of the members of the party traveled by horseback and camped often in the open, sometimes in Indian country. The trail led from East Texas through what is now the Dallas-Fort Worth area and westward along a line of frontier outposts including Fort Belknap, Phantom Hill and presumably to El Paso. They were greeted with enthusiasm in the towns in the settled areas.[8] In 1853, he supported the Gadsden Treaty in which the United States purchased from Mexico a strip of land west of El Paso for $10,000,000. Rusk believed

---

[6]Gammel, **Laws of Texas**, II, p. 1302.
[7]**State Gazette**, Austin, March 28, 1857.
[8]Rusk Papers, Thos. J. to David Rusk, Sept. 1853.

156

with President Pierce that this would clear the most practical route for the Pacific railroad. At every opportunity, he presented to the Federal government the advantages of the Southern route to California. President Pierce and Jefferson Davis, Secretary of War under that administration, also favored the Southern route. But for the Civil War, it might have been built with generous federal aid.

A popular practice of Congressmen was to send small packages or "papers" of garden and field seeds to their constituents. In February, 1856, Rusk sent seeds of two varieties of sweet sorghums, "China Sorghum Sugar Cane" and "Sorgo Sucre," which he thought would be valuable crops in Texas. What part, if any, these experimental seeds had in the development of the great sorghum grain crops of modern times is not learned.

However, there was a legend in the Rusk family that some of the experimental seeds which the Senator sent home did not turn out well. One year, the story goes, "David prepared a small field, planted it with seed that Tom had sent, tended it like a garden patch, and grew a fine crop of Johnson grass that nearly ruined the best part of his farm before he could get rid of it."[9]

During the days of the Republic, the services of General Rusk were immortalized in two geographical names on the Texas map. In 1843, a new county was created out of Nacogdoches County and was named Rusk. In later years a magnificent monument to the great soldier and statesman was erected in Henderson, the county seat. In 1846, the county of Cherokee was created out of Nacogdoches county and the county seat was named for Rusk.

<hr>

[9]Blount, p. 198.

CHAPTER 30

"Blessed Are the Pure in Heart"

Mary (Polly) Rusk was a home person. On only one occasion did she accompany her husband to Washington. At that time her health was breaking and social life in the capital was too much for her strength. She had become so frail that she could not struggle through the many changes of dress to meet the styles "and so confined herself to a pretty morning dress, open according to the fashion then prevailing, over an embroidered white petticoat, so as to be fashionable once a day."[1]

On this same tour, Mrs. Rusk and the Senator visited their relatives in Georgia and South Carolina, including Mary's parents, Gen. and Mrs. Benjamin Cleveland, and Rusk's mother, Mrs. Mary Rusk. His father, John Rusk, had died in 1844.

Health conditions in Texas during the days of the Republic and in the years following were extremely bad. Early deaths of most of the prominent people of the time indicate that the average life span was short. Aside from occasional outbreaks of cholera and yellow fever, there were the more common and on the whole more destructive diseases of tuberculosis, "billious fever" and malarial fever, the latter commonly called "chills and fever" or "every-other-day fever."

"The widespread prevalence of malaria, one of the chief deterrents to the development of the Texas wilderness, was a more consistently pressing problem than Indian and Mexican depredations," remarked William Ranson Hogan.[2] Mrs. Rusk was beset by this debilitating illness, carried by mosquitoes, probably on many occasions during the spring and summer months. One specific attack is mentioned in a letter in July 1850.[3]

The suffering caused by malarial fever is described in rhyme:

---

[1]Blount, p. 192-95.
[2]Hogan, p. 224.
[3]Rusk Papers, R. Parmalee to Rusk, July 13, 1850.

"Chills that set your bones to aching
Giving you an earthquake shaking,
Causing every tooth to chatter
Like bones shaken on a platter. . . ."[4]

(The author, having spent his childhood in East Texas, before the days of mosquito control, can testify that the description of the misery is not exaggerated.)

Possibly the weakening effect of malaria made Mrs. Rusk more susceptible to the more fatal disease of tuberculosis, which she acquired. Despite her frailty, Mary Rusk was the last to survive of a family of five. Her two brothers had died in young manhood, her sister, Mrs. Ann Thorn of Nacogdoches, died in June, 1855, and the other sister, Mrs. Catherine Hoyle, succumbed early in 1856.

Fearing she had not long to live, Mrs. Rusk planned with her husband a farewell trip to the home of her aging parents in Georgia—a bright dream of a fond reunion never to come to pass. While General Rusk was busy in the Senate in early spring, 1856, Mrs. Rusk became seriously ill. It was proposed to send for her husband, but she, with her usual spirit of sacrifice, refused to allow him to be called home. "He is where duty calls him," she said. "I do not wish him sent for until it is really necessary."[5]

Dr. J. H. Starr, rated as one of the outstanding physicians of Texas and a close friend of the family, wrote Senator Rusk on April 8 with ominous news: "Since writing you on the 5th, Mrs. Rusk's condition has materially changed for the worse. . . . Dr. Robert Irion said today he would write you . . . giving you his opinion as to her condition & the probable progress of her disease. For my own part, I confess my hopes are quite gone for anything more than temporary relief. Benjamin expresses a great desire for your immediate return & thinks his mother is anxious for it. I hope you will be able to do so.

"Of course all thought of the contemplated journey to Georgia is abandoned. This change taking place at this season of the year under a pleasant temperature causes me to apprehend that the warm season will prostrate instead of restoring her."[6]

---

[4]Hogan, p. 224.
[5]Cherokee Sentinel, Rusk, Texas, May 10, 1856, reprinted from Nacogdoches Chronicle, from copy in Rusk Papers.
[6]Rusk Papers, Dr. J. H. Starr to Rusk, April 8, 1856.

On the same day, Dr. Irion wrote, with somewhat less urgency, saying that Mrs. Rusk "may not be physically able" to make the proposed visit to her relatives in Georgia.[7]

But Mrs. Rusk sank so rapidly that there was no time for the doctors' letters to reach Washington by the slow means of transportation before the crisis came. Four days later a dispatch was sent by stage to New Orleans to be telegraphed from there, urging Rusk's immediate return. At the same time, Dr. Starr wrote a letter, though he did not expect it to reach Rusk before his departure for home: "Mrs. Rusk had a very bad night. . . . I fear she cannot last longer than a month. . . ."[8]

Had it been a month, the doctor's message via New Orleans thence by telegraph to Washington, might have reached Rusk in such time that, traveling in haste, he could have reached his wife's bedside. But it was not to be. Mary Rusk, courageous frontier wife, strong in spirit, was now frail in body. The dreadful disease was rapidly consuming her strength. She faced the ordeal without fear, surrounded by her children and cherished by her friends. There was one great sorrow—her life's companion could not be with her at the end.

Death came in the night—at two A.M., Saturday, April 26. She had lasted only two weeks of the month predicted in Dr. Starr's message. On Sunday, April 27, the lovely East Texas spring was in its glory—trees verdant in full leaf and flowers blooming in great profusion. It was a beautiful time to be laid to rest in the free soil of Texas for which she had lived the best part of her years. The Rev. Mr. Hayter pronounced a touching tribute to Mary Rusk. On that Sabbath morning, her children and a large concourse of friends in horsedrawn vehicles followed the hearse to the grave in Oak Grove Cemetery.

The honors achieved by Thomas J. Rusk must be shared equally by his wife, Mary. "Possessed of a practical and economical disposition, she became an invaluable aid to her husband," said the old *Nacogdoches Chronicle,* "and it was only by her arduous application to the affairs of the household that he was enabled to devote nearly all of the past twenty years to the service of his country. Impelled by a strong sense of duty,

---

[7]**Ibid.,** Dr. Robert Irion to Rusk, April 8, 1856.
[8]**Ibid.,** Dr. Starr to Rusk, April 12, 1856.

she has been ever ready to make any sacrifice, or endure any privation that he might be at the post of danger or duty."[9]

Among the graves of the heroes of the Texas Republic in Oak Grove Cemetery stands today the simple monument to Mary Rusk, provided by her husband, who ordered the inscription to read: *"Blessed are the pure in heart, for they shall see God."*

Senator Rusk arrived home to find his companion already in the grave. It was a shock and a loss from which he never was able to recover. Doubtless there was a feeling of remorse and an aching sense of regret that he had allowed his duty to country to separate him from his richest possession in the time of crisis.

Mrs. Rusk had borne for him seven children, two of whom died in infancy. Of the survivors, Benjamin Livingston Rusk now had a family of his own, having married a Nacogdoches girl, Rachel A. Crain, April 17, 1853. Rachel was a daughter of San Jacinto veteran, Roden T. Crain. Benjamin died in Austin in 1885. The lawyer son, John Cleveland Rusk, 26 at the time of his mother's death, had married Harriet Ann Patton, daughter of Capt. Robert S. Patton. His first wife died in 1860 and he married Cornelia E. Garrison of Cherokee County in 1862. He served ably in the army of the South in the Civil War. He died in 1898, being the last survivor of the children of Thomas J. and Mary Rusk.[10]

Cicero, the third surviving son of the Rusks, was 21 at the time of his Mother's death and still lived in the family home. When the Civil War erupted, he joined the Confederate Army and was killed in action. He was never married.

Two younger children survived their mother. Thomas David, a youth of 15 at the time, was in later years "a chip off the old block, a most affable man," according to Dr. J. E. Mayfield of San Antonio, a friend of the family. He died at Hallsville, Texas, in 1875, still a young man of 34.[11] Least but dearest, the only girl, Helena Argin, was left motherless at the age of 10. She, as well as young Tom, was placed in school by the father. Her life was short, death coming when she was about 18, reportedly following a fall from a horse.

---

[9]**Cherokee Sentinel,** Rusk, Texas, May 10, 1856, reprinted from **Nacogdoches Chronicle,** from copy in Rusk Papers.
[10]Sterrett, p. 195.
[11]Sterrett, p. 196.

CHAPTER 31

Higher Honors in Store

His spirit torn asunder by the tragedy of his wife's death, Thomas J. Rusk began a courageous effort to gather up the remnants. His first responsibility was to take charge of the younger children, Tom and Helena, who had been almost entirely the care of their mother. There were household affairs to be resolved as well as management of the slaves, who were considered almost a part of the family.

The house servant, Eunice, called affectionately "Aunt Dinny" by the family, and her slave husband, "Uncle Wiley," had been of great help in managing the home during Mrs. Rusk's illness and continued so after her death. They were especially devoted to little Helena and gave her tender care. "Aunt Dinny" had often accompanied Helena to the Old North Church, a non-denominational meeting house four miles north of town.

It is told that "Aunt Dinny," wearied almost to exhaustion with nursing Mrs. Rusk during her last illness, busied herself next day after the death, arranging pine boughs in the fireplace. She was urged to take her rest but replied: "O, no! This is Miss Polly's birthday in heaven."[1]

General Rusk did not return to Washington for the remainder of the session of Congress from which he had been summoned. He apologized for his absence in a letter to Gen. A. Anderson, July 29, 1856: "My situation for the last three months has been one of suspense and embarrassment. In addition to the remembrance of my irreparable calamity, my domestic affairs were in that condition that they required my personal attention. I am poor. I had left everything at home to another; that other has gone, hence my attention was necessary. I live near a little town and my two youngest children, a daughter of ten and a son of fifteen, required that care which it had been criminal in me to neglect."[2]

---

[1]Blount, p. 185.
[2]Rusk Papers, Rusk to Gen. A. Anderson, July 29, 1856.

As ever, Rusk was torn between his duties to his country and his responsibility to his family. He had determined to return to Washington, taking the two children with him. Just as he was able to start, he learned that Congress had set the date for adjournment and would be in session only a few days after he could make the journey, requiring two weeks or longer.

Besides, Helena had been ill and the father was apprehensive of the children's health on the long trip during the summer season. Apparently he was concerned somewhat for his own health as in his letter to General Anderson, he used the words, "If I should live," in connection with his plans for the autumn.

The letter to Anderson concerned railroad legislation, affecting the proposed Pacific Railroad by the southern route for which Rusk had labored through the years and which was destined to remain his unfinished task. "I think it would be bad policy to press any important measure at this session," Rusk advised. "The black Republicans in the House are bent solely upon Presidential capital and a struggle for power and would defeat any measure that did not favor them. The next session will be the important one for good or evil. The election will be out of the way and measures will then stand more fairly on their merits. If I should live, I hope to be upon the ground early."[3]

Senator Houston about this time was also concerned about the rising strength of the new Republican Party. "I dread the success of the Black Republicans," he wrote Rusk. However, the Democrats were to elect one more President. Neither Rusk nor Houston, both of whom had been prominent in the 1852 convention, were on hand for the 1856 Democratic meeting in Cincinnati, where James Buchanan was nominated for President and John C. Breckenridge for Vice-President. Possibly their absence contributed to rumors that neither Texas Senator would return for the fall session of Congress.

L. L. Lewis was writing Rusk, urging him to throw off his depression and return to Washington with General Houston, bringing Tom and Helena with him.[4] Whether he was influenced by the plea from Lewis or not, that was what Rusk determined to do. He proposed to Houston that they make the trip to Washington together, but Houston sent his regrets that "it will not be in my power to go with you . . . though I would be de-

---

[3]Ibid.
[4]Rusk Papers, L. L. Lewis to Rusk, June 14 and 17, 1856.

163

lighted to do so. Mrs. Houston enjoys so little health that I am distressed. I suffer much from my San Jacinto wound & am quite lame. Otherwise, I am hardy as a bear. . . . I will try & get off, if Mrs. Houston's situation will allow on the 15th November. . . . We were once young, but now old! ! !"[5] Strange words in view of the fact that Houston was to run for Governor a few months later.

In the same letter, Houston expressed his concern for Rusk's children. He had learned that Tom and Helena were to accompany their father to Washington. Concerning Helena, he wrote: "I do pray you to pre select where you place her at school, and I almost claim of you to see Mrs. Smith near Boston; if you are pleased, place here there. Or if not there, at some institution in Virginia. . . . I hope we will have an opportunity of conversing on this subject as I deem it a matter of importance."[6]

Just what school Helena attended is not clear, but she was not altogether happy—possibly homesick. "I have Tom in a writing school where he has improved considerably and shall start him to a regular school after the first of January," Rusk wrote to David. "He is well contented and says he is willing to remain at school for three years. Helena is going to school but is not so well contented and insists on being back home in the spring."[7]

Rusk had plunged into his busy rounds in the Senate. He secured the repeal of a law which had been passed in his absence at the former session limiting the time at which those having claims against Texas might present them at the treasury to January 1, 1856, and providing that the money left should be divided among the creditors who had already been paid. His new bill extended the time to January, 1858. "This met with streneous opposition and the creditors who had been paid and expected another grab used every effort to defeat me, but my bill passed the Senate" 35 to 9.[8] It was the final battle in Rusk's long fight for just settlement of the Texas debt.

In the Presidential election of 1856, Rusk continued his loyalty to the Democratic Party, supporting the Buchanan ticket. But Houston made speeches in Texas and elsewhere in

---

[5]Houston to Rusk from Huntsville, Nov. 8, 1856.
[6]Ibid.
[7]Rusk Papers, Thos J. to David Rusk, Dec. 21, 1856.
[8]Ibid.

behalf of the "Know-Nothing (American) Party candidate, former President Fillmore. The two Senators engaged in a friendly debate in Nacogdoches on September 16, each defending his own political position, but at the same time paying each other warm personal compliments. Reversing the usual role of the two speakers, Houston was comparatively mild in his attacks on Buchanan, but Rusk barred no holds in his assault on Fillmore. The outcome of the election sounded the death knell for the "Know-Nothing" movement, but at the same time revealed the declining power of the Democratic Party. Though Buchanan won with 174 electoral votes, the new party which the Texas Senators called the "black Republicans" counted 114 votes for their candidate, J. C. Fremont. Fillmore received only eight.

The popularity of Rusk reached new heights at this time. In his home state, Texas, he was without a peer. In the Senate, his seniority of ten years, coupled with his ability and personal popularity, gave him an enviable position of influence. His outstanding service as chairman of the Post Office Committee for several years, made him a natural prospect for Postmaster General in the new Cabinet. President Buchanan was said to have offered him the Cabinet post, but Rusk declined. Since the death of his wife, he was growing even more reticent than in the past.

Nevertheless, there was again talk of Thomas J. Rusk for the presidency of the United States. There was a hope among some of the statesmen of the time, probably forlorn, that he might have bridged the chasm which was dividing the nation had he lived longer. Senator Seward spoke of him as "one for whom I thought higher honors were preparing . . . who seemed to me to stand a monument against which the waves of faction must break . . . with whom I thought I might do so much, and without whom I could do almost nothing to magnify the honor of the Republic."[9] And R. W. Stayton remarked that had Rusk lived until "the disaffection of the two wings of the Democratic party in the next campaign, that perhaps there would have been no parting of the ways."[10]

As the session of Congress drew near the close, the esteem

---

[9]Speech of Senator William H. Seward in United States Senate, January 19, 1858, leaflet in Texas State Archives, also **Congressional Globe**, that date, pp. 332-33.
[10]Stayton, p. 26.

165

in which Rusk was held in the Senate was manifested in his election as President Pro-Tempore by a large majority. For a short time, until the close of the session on March 14, he presided over the Senate. It was doubtless a source of elation to occupy the seat which had been filled by his mentor, Vice President John C. Calhoun, during Rusk's first association with the great Southerner some 30 years before.

Rusk was fully recognized at that time as "a man of rare qualities." The distinguished historian, Hubert Howe Bancroft in an unbiased appraisal, describes him as a "statesman of high order, energetic, and possessed of a mind of great clearness and strength." And continues:

> "Of remarkably sound judgment, supported by wide experience, he [Rusk] had an accurate and extensive knowledge of mankind. And his wisdom and talents were equalled by his virtues—courage, honesty, and truth . . . Insensible to adulation, he never stooped to flattery. In his intercourse with men he did not affect dignified importance, but was accessible to all; and it was a habit of his to converse with men in the humblest stations of life as freely as with those of the highest, while his sympathy for the unfortunate or oppressed, and his love of justice and candor won for him the respect and affections of every class. Uninfluenced by selfish motives and by personal ambition, he labored in the Senate for the aggrandizement of the nation at large, and the promotion of the general welfare."[11]

To Bancroft's assessment must be added that, in public life, his first loyalty was to Texas, and he was ever alert to defend the interests of the state he loved.

Depressed as he was at this time, Rusk could readily sympathize with an old friend who had known better days. Came a message from Mirabeau B. Lamar, "in pecuniary distress," seeking an appointment as "resident minister to some of the European or South American Republics, or would accept the Governorship of a Territory." Rusk signed a letter to President Buchanan who appointed the former Texas President and war hero as minister to Nicaragua and Costa Rica.[12]

The lines of the old guard of the Texas Revolution and

---

[11]Bancroft, Hubert Howe, **History of the North Mexican States and Texas** (The History Company, Publishers, San Francisco, 1889) II, pp. 421-22.
[12]Lamar Papers, Rusk letter from Washington to H. A. Wise, Richmond, Va., March 6, 1857, Texas State Library.

Republic were growing thin. Besides the heroes who had fallen in battle such as Fannin, Bowie, Travis, Crockett and Milam, others like Austin had succumed to disease. An appalling number, like the sad denounment of an ancient Greek tragedy, had died at their own hands. Looking back over the years, Peter W. Grayson, candidate for President of the Republic in 1838 had shot himself. Chief Justice Collingsworth, who succeeded him as candidate, leaped from a steamer and drowned in Galveston Bay. George C. Childress, author of the Texas Declaration of Independence, took his own life. Looking ahead, Anson Jones, the last President of the Republic, politically disappointed, blew out his brains at the old Capitol Hotel in Houston in January, 1858. Thomas J. Rusk was drawn in that direction. He could not throw off the melancholia that possessed him.

After winding up affairs at the close of Congress, Senator Rusk departed Washington for the last time. He was accompanied home by Helena. Spring came late to the Redlands that year, 1857. The usual beauty of trees and flowers was slow in emerging; planting of crops was late and the country was drab even in April when Rusk arrived home. The house, empty of Mary Rusk's presence, was gloomy and depressing, adding to Rusk's melencholia. Besides, he was sick of body as well as of spirit. His illness grew serious and recovery was slow. He kept much to himself and brooded over his loss. His family and close friends could not stir him out of his depression.

He developed a painful boil on the back of his neck, adding to his misery. Bancroft referred to it as a tumor and thought it might have affected Rusk's mind.[13] It was generally agreed that he was mentally ill.

An old friend, John H. Reagan, then in the U. S. House of Representatives, spoke of Rusk's bereavement and "many cares and perplexities" and said, "to these were added a disease which . . . may have affected his spine and brain. And these combined causes, operating upon his keenly sensitive mental organization . . . caused his reason to give way."[14]

---

[13]Bancroft, p. 421.
[14]**Congressional Globe**, Jan. 19. 1858, 35th Cong., 1st Session, p. 336.

CHAPTER 32

A Destiny Fulfilled

Thomas J. Rusk rose at his usual hour on Wednesday morning, July 29. James L. Smith, a friend of Cicero, was visiting in the home. The General remarked that he was feeling better than he had for some time. He had visited casually with Dr. James H. Starr the day before and told the physician that he planned to ride some every day. Dr. Starr noted that he looked less gloomy and was in a better humor than he had usually been of late.

During the morning Wednesday, he remarked that he was going squirrel hunting, and Cicero remembered seeing him loading his rifle, carefully pouring the powder down the barrel, inserting the wadding and the bullet, and packing down the load with the ramrod.

At lunch, he talked as usual, but ate little. Smith remembered later that the General ate only a little rice and drank some milk. Later, he entered the room where Cicero and Smith were resting on the bed, and inquired of Cicero if he were sick. Cicero assured his father he was well. He and Smith were planning a ride and had sent a slave to the pasture for horses. Rusk went out and spoke to the negro man, asking where he was going, and the slave replied that he was ordered by Cicero to fetch horses.

A few minutes later, Rusk was seen crossing the back yard from the cabin occupied by the negro, Wiley, to the main house. In five minutes a muffled shot was heard by Cicero and Smith. Upon investigation, they found the body of General Rusk near the back door. Jesse Lee testified that the General was lying on his right side, his right hand grasping the gun near the muzzle, "the gun lying by him on his right side also, with a string tied to the trigger and under his right hand." Dr. Starr said a wound in his head, "I have no doubt, produced instant death."[1]

---

[1]Original record of inquest in the death of Thomas J. Rusk on July 29, 1857 (filed July 31) now in Special Collections, Stephen F. Austin State

Justice of Peace William F. Hyde summoned a jury composed of W. B. Ochiltree, John T. Shanks, H. H. Edwards, John W. Crain, Richard J. Walker and John S. Roberts. After the testimony of Dr. Starr, Smith, Lee and Cicero Rusk, the jury returned the verdict that death was caused by a gun shot wound "in the fore part of the head inflicted by a shot from a rifle gun held in his own hands & discharged by himself."[2]

Thomas J. Rusk had joined the tragic band of Texas patriots in suicide. It was the culmination of a year of grief over his wife's death. His last duty had been in her memory. The only writing he left that fateful day was a letter addressed to a monument dealer in New Orleans:

> "Dear Sir: Will you be kind enough to send me to care of James H. Starr a neat head stone for a grave with these words upon it
> Mary Rusk
> Born August 1809
> Died April 26, 1856
> Blessed are the pure in heart
> for they shall see God.
> If the money in your hands is not sufficient to pay for it, draw upon Dr. Starr for any balance.
> Truly yours
> Tho. J. Rusk"
> "Eneas Smith, Esq."[3]

These were the last lines that Rusk ever wrote. His handwriting did not falter. There was no other final message and he left no will as far as records show. His death, described by news reports as a great mystery, was hardly a mystery at all. The sad facts tell the story of a tortured, broken spirit.

One wonders where little Helena, the most cherished one after the loss of his wife, was on that tragic day. Mercifully, she seems to have been away from home—possibly her father arranged it that way—but no record shows her whereabouts. The youthful Tom was in school in Murfreesboro, Tenn., and wrote frequently to his father, with encouraging reports, apparently realizing his parent's need for encouragement. Some

University Library, Nacogdoches. Miss Mildred Wyatt is director of the Special Collections which contain a large amount of valuable materials concerning Rusk. Miss Wyatt was most helpful in making these materials available to the author.

[2]Record of Inquest.

[3]Copy in Special Collections, SFA Library.

three weeks before his father's death, Tom wrote an enthusiastic letter, saying his school report was "very good." He was one of the most devoted of the Rusk children.

There came to light among Rusk's papers a lament which the bereaved father had written more than twenty years before—reflections upon the death of his two-year old son and namesake, Thomas Jefferson Rusk, Jr. It closed with the words, "You've left this world of sin and sorrow first—It will not be long till we shall follow you and mingle with the cold and silent dust."[4] Many years and mighty events had intervened, but the destiny was now fulfilled. And while the body mingled with the dust, the kindly spirit and the great service for Texas and the nation survived as a living memorial to a good and great man.

The shock which reverberated in the State and Nation at the death of Thomas J. Rusk is reflected in his home paper. "A great calamity has befallen the State of Texas," proclaimed the *Nacogdoches Chronicle*. One of her most distinguished and noblest sons has fallen. Thomas J. Rusk is no more.

> "A gloom hangs over the people; a mystery, thus far, is connected with the matter. We can only give the facts and mourn the sad stroke which has thus deprived Texas and the South of a valued and useful champion.
>
> Gen. Rusk has, ever since the death of his lady, suffered under a mental depression. . . . He has, to a great extent, secluded himself from society, and lately that despondancy has been more marked and apparent to those familiar with him. A severe illness from which he was just recovering, had prostrated him for weeks. . . . Let the people mourn the loss of a man who on the field of battle and in the Councils of the State and Nation, has proved himself to be worthy the proud place already accorded him in the affections of the people."[5]

A Nacogdoches youth viewed the fallen body of Rusk and carried with him through life the morbid picture. Dr. J. S. Mayfield wrote in later years: "I was only a boy, fourteen years old, at the time of his death . . . and he was then about sixty years old [actually 53]. I saw him many times, from that point of view, and also saw him lying upon the ground just as he fell."[6]

---

[4]Rusk Papers.
[5]**Nacogdoches Chronicle,** July 31, 1857.
[6]Sterrett, p. 198.

Through most of his life, Rusk was pinched by poverty, plagued by debts and besieged by pleas by others for financial aid. He was generous to his mother and to his in-laws when they were in need, sometimes depriving himself and his own family. By the time of his death, he had attained financial security and accumulated a modest estate, though his cash assets and income were never large, even by standards of the times.

Original documents in the County Clerk's Office at Nacogdoches show that Dr. James H. Starr and N. J. Moore were named as appraisers and valued the property as:

Lands and Land Claims	$29,433.00
Negroes	11,500.00
Personal Property (Live- stock, Farm Equipment, etc.)	3,062.00
Library	934.00
Crops and Money	1,999.22
Total	46,928.22

The appraisal was filed November 7, 1857. A commission composed of Dr. Starr along with David Muckleroy and Daniel Atkins was appointed to divide the property evenly between the five heirs, taking into account certain property which had already been given to the older sons, Benjamin and John. Benjamin was named guardian for Tom and Helena. John, the lawyer, was named administrator.

It is interesting to note that only $614.22 in money was listed in the assets. There were 20 slaves, men, women and children, ranging in age from a boy, Frank, 2, and upward to 55. The house maid, Eunice, and her fiddling husband, "Uncle" Wiley, were awarded to Helena. The slaves were valued according to age and sex. Eunice, age 52, was appraised at $200, while a young man, Aaron, 35, was valued at $1,200, and two-year-old Frank at $300. The appraisers could not foresee that before Frank was old enough for work, he and all the others would be free and the value of $11,500 put upon them would be "gone with the wind" on emancipation.

Other items in the property inventory are of some interest. There was the Rusk library of a thousand volumes, including works of Chesterfield, Macaulay, Gibbons, Jefferson,

Adams, Hamilton and Webster, evidence of Rusk's absorbing interest in history and politics. A "painting by Stanley," subject not named, was valued at $3.25.

Listed in the personal property was "one fine walking cane presented from friends in California $75," another "fine walking cane from the Old Constitution $10, and "one common walking cane $1." Named also was a pair of dueling pistols, $40 and a Sharps Rifle $10.

Farm equipment, typical of the times, included a two-horse wagon, another large horse wagon and "old gears," a large ox-wagon and a buggy and harness. Livestock on hand indicated there was more ranching than farming on the "Santo Domingo:" 150 head of cattle, 200 hogs, two horses and five mules. But there was a considerable amount of farm products in the Rusk barns: 1700 bushels of corn, 5000 bundles of fodder, 20 bushels of rye and ten of peas.

Twenty-eight tracts of land, scattered over eastern Texas, owned in whole or part, were included in the Rusk property. Acreages were listed in the counties of Nacogdoches, Angelina, Cherokee, Henderson, Hopkins, Kaufman, Houston, Upshur, Cook and as far west as Bexar County.[7] Land values were very low, much of the acreage was acquired as bounties or bought for 50 cents an acre. It was years before it would bring good prices and be highly profitable for farming and stock-raising.

In the final settlement of the estate, filed March 2, 1860, the value of the property was shown to be considerably more than the first appraisal. Each of the five heirs received $11,-581.28, making the total $57,906.40.[8] Part of this difference might have been accounted for by "other property held jointly with Gen. J. P. Henderson," mentioned but not appraised in an earlier report by John C. Rusk, administrator.

[7]Original Documents, County Clerk's Office, Nacogdoches, Texas
[8]Ibid.

CHAPTER 33

"His Name Belongs to History"

General Rusk was buried in Oak Grove Cemetery beside the grave of his wife and among the sepulchers of a host of heroic Texas men. In the famous burying ground are the tombs of four signers of the Texas Declaration of Independence and a number of the heroes who fought for Texas freedom, some of them Rusk's comrades at San Jacinto. Names on the gravestones read like a rollcall of patriots of the Lone Star: Charles S. Taylor, John S. Roberts, William S. Clark and Thomas J. Rusk, all signers of the Declaration. Among the veterans of San Jacinto buried here, besides Rusk, are Capt. Hayden Arnold, Thomas Y. Buford, Elias E. Hamilton and David Rusk. There are other prominent soldiers and patriots, such as Hayden Edwards, leader of the Fredonian Rebellion; Kelsey H. Douglass, commander in the battles against the Cherokees; John Forbes, Adolphus Sterne and Dr. Robert A. Irion. All these were once companions of Thomas J. Rusk.

"No man ever served in public life more entirely free from even the suspicion of corrupt, mercenary, or improper motives," declared Judge John Hemphill, Chief Justice of the Texas Supreme Court, in his eulogy in the Texas House of Representatives. Judge Hemphill knew Rusk personally as a friend and law associate. He had served as one of the justices in the first session of the Supreme Court of the Texas Republic—the session over which Rusk presided as Chief Justice. In his address, Hemphill reviewed the service of Rusk to the Republic, the State and the Nation, and continued: "With integrity, purity and singleness of purpose, he devoted his great talents to his country, unswerved by selfish designs or the impulses of ill-regulated ambition."

Judge Hemphill saw in Rusk a charisma which made him a leader of men, saying in his address:

"He was largely endowed with that fine electric quality which seems the gift of nature—the result, perhaps, of a rare combination of the higher qualities of intellect and of the heart, which inspires confidence, and exerts in a mystical way, a control over surrounding persons, which exacts obedience from a soldier more from attachment and a high and implicit trust, than from the force of discipline, which in the hour of danger, draws all to him as the pilot who must weather the storm; which arbitrates and settles the difficulties of others, makes friends everywhere without effort, and in legislative assemblies, gives an influence which no mere talent, intellect, energy or efforts to please can ever possess. . . .

"He has left us a bright heritage of Liberties won by his valor and sustained . . . by the wisdom of his councils. . . ." the speaker remarked, adding, "His place may be filled, but who can fill the void in the hearts of his countrymen?"[1]

J. Pinckney Henderson, ex-Governor and General Rusk's former law partner, was elected by the Legislature to fill the vacancy in the United States Senate. He was ill and unable to be present when Congress convened in the fall. In fact he served only a short time before his death in June the following year. Anson Jones, who had coveted the office of Senator when Rusk was first elected in 1846, aspired to succeed Rusk in 1857 but was again disappointed.

Houston left the Senate in 1859 to serve as Governor of Texas and was succeeded by Judge Hemphill. It would be many years before men of the distinction of Rusk and Houston would represent Texas in the United States Senate. The line of succession, though interrupted by the period of the Confederacy, can be traced to the present time. In the Houston line were such men as Joseph W. Bailey, Morris Sheppard, Lyndon Johnson and, at present, John G. Tower. Rusk's successors included Roger Q. Mills, Charles A. Culberson, Tom Connally and Ralph W. Yarborough.

When Congress convened in December, following Rusk's death, Senator Houston had planned to introduce the new Senator, Henderson, and at the same time pay tribute to the one deceased. However, when Henderson was unable to attend, Houston proceeded on January 19, 1858, to pay tribute to his colleague and friend. He reviewed briefly the life of Thomas J. Rusk and the service he had given to Texas and the nation,

---

[1]Hemphill, p. 29.

a service in many respects parallel to Houston's own, during the 23 years from the time the two met in Nacogdoches.

"His fame is national, not sectional. His name belongs to history. . . . He stood conspicious in everything that was good and great. He was a man whose influence was felt throughout the nation; nor was the wound unfelt that inflicted his death." Houston continued in eloquent tribute:

> "Sir, we may say of him . . . that as a soldier he was gallant his chivalry spotless, his honor clear: as a states-man he was wise, considerate, and patriotic; as a friend he had all the high qualities that enoble the heart; as a father he was affectionate almost to infirmity; as a hus-band, he was manly, noble and erect; as a man, he had all the qualities that adorn human nature; and if he had in-firmities, they were few in proportion to those which fall to the lot of man. He will be remembered here; he will be remembered thoughout the nation; he will be unfor-gotten in Texas whilst either history or tradition lives. Texas had lost one of the bright and staunch pillars of her edifice; and she has no material [with which] to re-place him in this body."[2]

At the conclusion of his eulogy, Senator Houston offered a resolution, "That the members of the Senate, from a sincere desire of showing every mark of respect due to the memory of the Hon. Thomas J. Rusk, deceased, . . . will go into mourning, by wearing crepe on the left arm for thirty days," and as an additional mark of respect that the senate adjourn.[3]

Senator Collamer of Vermont and Senator Gwin of Califor-nia supported the resolutions with "great feeling and eloquence," but it remained for Senator William H. Seward of New York, Rusk's personal admirer and political adversary, to pay the most poignant tribute. "It is true," said Seward, "that I was not his kinsman, nor his neighbor, nor even his political associate. I was nevertheless, attached to him by bonds strong as the charity that consecrates even those relations. . . . I was his captive; an adversary, overpowered, overcome and conquered by his gener-osity . . . released on parole, a prisoner at large, but devoted to him by gratitude for the period of my whole life."[4]

With a rare perception, Seward was able to understand the

---

[2]Houston's Writings, VI, pp. 465-66.
[3]Congressional Globe, Jan. 19, 1858, p. 331.
[4]Ibid., pp. 332-33, also leaflet of Seward speech in Texas State Archives.

character of Rusk, to appreciate his greatness and to analyze the reasons for the Texas Senator's rise to a position of power and influence. "He knew no fear of opposition," explained the New York Senator. "As he was without fear, so he was also free from jealousy and from envy. . . . He despised art, trick and cunning and advanced directly toward his appointed end."

Allowing that Rusk was sometimes irritated at "Seeming injustice, or misapprehension," Seward added: "I doubt whether any setting sun, during his whole life, ever witnessed his anger." In a personal lament, he said, "Farewell, noble patriot, heroic soldier, faithful statesman, generous friend! loved by no means the least, although among the last of friends secured."[5]

The resolution for a season of mourning and immediate adjournment was unanimously adopted by the Senate. To Congressman John H. Reagan of Texas went the honor of introducing companion resolutions in the House of Representatives. Reagan recalled that Rusk, in the days of the Republic, when the Presidency "was at his command, without opposition, . . . declined to accept it," and had recently "refused the use of his name for the Vice Presidency of the United States, and has repeatedly discouraged the mention of his name for the Presidency."

Reagan concluded his eulogy with a personal note:

> "I speak here, not only as the representative of the district in which General Rusk has lived, ever since his immigration to Texas; but, as one who has seen him in his home, with his family, around his own fireside, amongst his neighbors, in the court-house, on the tented field and in the blazing front of battle; the same pure and just, and generous and noble man . . . more worthy of imitation, in his leading characteristics, than any other it has been my fortune to know."[6]

Congressman Keitt of South Carolina spoke in behalf of the state in which Rusk was born and in which his mother still lived, mentioning that one of the Senator's last acts was to "secure a few homely comforts to his aged mother." Mr. Jackson of Georgia added his voice of praise for the patriot who had lived for a few years in that state. He mentioned the aged parents of Mrs. Rusk, General and Mrs. Benjamin Cleveland,

---

[5]Ibid.
[6]Congressional Globe, Jan. 19, 1858, p. 336.

saying, "The last prop which held them up has been sundered: and soon they, too, must totter and fall."[7]

"He was a southern man: but . . . he employed the labors of his life to give strength and life to the American Union," spoke Representative Clark of New York State. "Like other statesmen of America, while representing in our Senate the special interests of a southern State, his comprehension was large enough, and his patriotism was warm enough, to enable him to uphold and strengthen the pillars of the Republic."[8]

The House adopted the resolutions of mourning and adjourned. Thus, for an interlude, there was rare harmony in Congress. North and South, East and West, had joined in grieving the loss of an American statesman whom all could admire.

---

[7]Ibid.
[8]Ibid., p. 338.

CHAPTER 34

"He Lived for Texas"

Insofar as the history books are concerned, Rusk has been sadly neglected. Though recognized during his lifetime as one of the greatest men of Texas, he has, in the present generation, been all but forgotten. Mention Thomas J. Rusk to the average Texas college graduate and you get the response, "Who was he?" However, there are some imposing memorials commemorating his service for Texas and the Nation.

Probably the first official rememberance is a portrait of Rusk painted by Willian Henry Huddle which was unveiled in the Senate Chamber of the Texas Capitol in 1889. The 20th Legislature appropriated $1,000 to pay for the painting, which still hangs in the Senate Chamber.

The most imposing monument is that at Henderson, county seat of Rusk County, which was named for the statesman. It consists of a tall, granite shaft crested by a lifesize bronze statue of General Rusk. The monument formerly stood in the center of the public square but became a traffic hazard and was moved to the front of the Courthouse lawn.

The memorial faces east and on the front reads: "Thomas Jefferson Rusk, December fifth, 1803, July twenty-ninth, 1857. Soldier, Patriot, Jurist, Statesman."

The west face reads: "He signed the Declaration of Independence, helped draft the Constitution. To a large degree, he devised the Court System and served as Chief Justice of the Republic of Texas."

On the north side: "Bold, intrepid and daring on the field of battle, he is yet more honored for wise forbearance and sound judgment. His able counsel as Secretary of War materially assisted in the winning of freedom for Texas."

On the south face: "Strong advocate for annexation—he presided over the Convention of 1845 which framed the first State Constitution and as United States Senator, he was foremost in the settlement of the Rio Grande as the boundary of Texas."

In Nacogdoches, where Rusk lived throughout his career in Texas, suitable memorials were long delayed, but today there are many reminders of the town's most honored citizen. A plaque marks the site of the family home on North Street on the hill which overlooks the beautiful Stephen F. Austin State University campus. The University people are proud of the fact that part of the campus is a portion of the former Rusk plantation. One of the handsome buildings is named for Thomas J. Rusk, and at the reconstructed Old Stone Fort an upstairs room has been designated as the Rusk Room. Here are displayed some historical relics, including a massive poster bed used by the General. Among the mementos is the family bible. There are pictures of Rusk, his wife, Mary, and his brother, David, and tenderly preserved, a lock of the General's hair. Other relics in the room are typical of the times in which Rusk lived, among them an old spinning wheel. There is a trunk found in a buried cellar uncovered on the campus, but its contents do not reveal to whom it belonged.

The grave site in Oak Grove cemetery fell into neglect. The matter was brought to public attention by the Nacogdoches *Star News*: "In an obscure part of the Nacogdoches cemetery, covered only by a rotten shelter of shingles, latticed in on the sides, is the grave of Rusk, neglected and forgotten by the people of Texas, the beneficiaries of his labor. Up to a short time ago, this rotten wooden shelter was a 'hogs' bed'. Even the mound of clay had been rooted away from the grave of one who presided over the chief legislative body of the United States: who led the army of Texas in her fearful struggle for liberty...."[1]

Evidently sentiment was aroused and around 1893 the Texas Legislature appropriated $1,000 for erection of a monument at the grave. A committee of Nacogdoches citizens was authorized to design the memorial and attend to its erection. The result of their efforts is a stately granite obelisk which stands at the grave, visible from the adjacent street. It was unveiled September 21, 1894. The monogram "R" is inscribed on the sides of the monument. On one side is the Seal of the State of Texas and the words: "Patriot, Soldier, Statesman, Jurist."

---

[1]Clipping from **Star News** (Nacogdoches) in Special Collections, SFA Library, date missing.

Inscription on another side reads: "Erected by the State of Texas to the memory of General Thomas J. Rusk, who fought for her liberty at San Jacinto. Born in South Carolina, December 5, 1808 [should be 1803], died in Nacogdoches, Texas, July 29, 1857." "HE LIVED FOR TEXAS."

Unlike his distinguished Texas contemporary, Sam Houston, who was deposed as Governor and ostracized during the Civil War, Rusk died at the height of his fame. No one can say his work was done. A few weeks before his death, he had confided to John H. Reagan that he "looked with fearful apprehension" upon the "alarming agitation of the question of slavery, as tending to weaken his high hopes of the future destiny of the Republic." At that time, according to Reagan, Rusk "was considering with great anxiety whether any means could be adopted which would avert these dangers, and secure . . . that fraternal good feelings, and mutual respect for the rights of others, which should ever characterize the people of a nation so blessed with all the elements of happiness and prosperity as our own."[2]

But neither Rusk nor the small remnant of other wise and unselfish statesmen of the time could stem the torrent of hatred and rashness which plunged the nation into disaster. Had Rusk lived, he would have faced the bitter choice between loyalty to the Nation he had served with honor, and love for the State which he had fought to liberate and had fostered from a wilderness to a growing empire.

Though he was a slave-owner, the emancipation of the slaves would to him have been no overriding issue. But just as Robert E. Lee must cast his lot with his native Virginia, so Rusk undoubtedly would have followed his beloved Texas in secession. Death saved him the great sorrow of the baptism of blood, so senseless, yet so inevitable, that neither he nor heaven itself could forstall.

---

[2]Congressional Globe, Jan. 19, 1858, p. 336.

Bibliography

Bancroft, Hubert Howe, *History of North Mexican States and Texas*, The History Co., San Francisco, 1889.

Barker, Eugene C., *Texas History*, Southwest Press, Dallas, 1929.

Barker, Eugene C., *The San Jacinto Campaign*, in *Texas State Historical Association Quarterly*, Vol. IV, April, 1901, Austin.

Bassett, John Spencer, *A Short History of the United States*, The Macmillan Co., New York, 1914.

Binkley, William C., Ed. *Official Correspondence of the Texas Revolution, 1835-1836*, D. Appleton-Century Co., New York, 1936.

Blount, Lois Foster, *A Brief History of Thomas J. Rusk Based on His Letters to His Brother, David, 1835-1856*, in *Southwestern Historical Quarterly*, Vol XXXIV, Austin, 1931.

Brooks, Elizabeth, *Prominent Women of Texas*, The Werner Co., Akron, Ohio, 1896.

Brown, John Henry, *The Encyclopedia of the New West.*

Brown, John Henry, *History of Texas, 1685 to 1892*, L. E. Daniell, Publisher, St. Louis, 1892.

Congressional Globe, Washington, D.C., from bound volumes in Hardin-Simmons University Library, Abilene, Texas.

Cherokee Sentinel, Rusk, Texas, May 10, 1856.

Crittenden, J. J., Letter to Thos. J. Rusk, in *Texana*, Waco, Texas.

Dallas Morning News, Aug. 15, 1942.

District Court Minutes, District Clerk's Office, Court House, Nacogdoches, Texas.

Foote, Henry Stuart, *Texas and Texans*, Thomas, Cowperthwait & Co., Philadelphia, 1841.

Ford, John Salmon, *Rip Ford's Texas*, Ed. by Oates, Stephen B., University of Texas Press, Austin, 1963.

Fowler, Littleton, *The Old Journal of*, in *Texas State Historical Association Quarterly*, Vol. II.

Friend, Llerena, *Sam Houston, the Great Designer*, University of Texas Press, Austin, 1954.

Galveston Weekly News, Sept. 15, 1857, General Sherman's Letter.

Gambrell, Herbert, *Anson Jones, the Last President of Texas*, annotated edition, University of Texas Press, Austin, 1964.

Gammel, H. P. N., *Laws of Texas*, Austin, 1898.

Gray, William F., *Diary, From Virginia to Texas, 1835*, Gray, Dillaye & Co., Houston, 1909.

Gulick, Charles Adams, Jr., Ed., *Papers of Mirabeau Bounaparte Lamar*, Texas State Library, Austin.

Hemphill, John, *Eulogy of the Life and Character of Thomas Jefferson Rusk*, delivered in House of Representatives Austin, 1857. From a copy in Stephen F. Austin State University Library, Nacogdoches.

Hogan, William Ranson, *The Republic of Texas*, University of Oklahoma Press, Norman, 1946.

Anonymous, *The Life of Sam Houston, the Only Authentic Memoir of Him Ever Published*, J. C. Derby, New York, 1855.

Inquest in Death of Thomas J. Rusk, July 29, 1857. Original document in Special Collections, Stephen F. Austin State University Library.

James, Marquis, *The Raven, a Biography of Sam Houston*, Cop. 1929 by Marquis James, 1956 by Jacqueline Mary Parsons James, by permission of the Publishers, The Bobbs-Merrill Co.

Jaynes, R. T., *Thomas Jefferson Rusk*, privately published, Walhalla, S. C., 1944.

Journals of the House of Representatives, Third Congress, Republic of Texas, 1838.

Kemp, Louis Wiltz, *The Signers of the Texas Declaration of Independence*, The Anson Jones Press, Salado, Texas, 1959.

Lebadie, Dr. N. D., *The Battle of San Jacinto*, published in *Texas Almanac*, 1859.

Lubbock, Francis R., *Six Decades in Texas or Memoirs*, Austin, 1900.

McDonald, Archie P., Ed., *Hurrah for Texas! The Diary of Adolphus Sterne*, Texian Press, Waco, 1969.

Middleton, Annie Irene, *The Texas Convention of 1845*, in *Southwestern Historical Quarterly*, Vol. XXV.

Nacogdoches Archives, Texas State Library, Austin, also printed volumes in Stephen F. Austin State University Library.

Nance, Joseph Milton, *After San Jacinto*.

Probate Court Records and Deed Records, County Clerk's Office, Nacogdoches, Texas.

Reagan, John H., *Expulsion of the Cherokees from East Texas*, in *Texas State Historical Association Quarterly*, Vol. I, Austin.

Red River Patriot, Shreveport, La., March 15, 1839.

Rusk Papers, University of Texas Archives, Austin.

Rusk, Thomas J., Speech on *The Texas Debt*, in U.S. Senate, July 19, 1854. Leaflet in Texas State Library.

Seward, William H., *Remarks in Memory of Thomas J. Rusk*, in U. S. Senate, Washington, 1858. Leaflet in Texas State Archives.

Special Collections, Stephen F. Austin State University Library, Thomas J. Rusk Files.

Spillman, W. J., *Adjustment of the Texas Boundary in 1850*, in *Texas State Historical Association Quarterly*, Vol. VII.

Stayton, R. W., Address on *Thomas J. Rusk* before the Texas Bar Association, *Texas Law Review*, October, 1925.

Sterrett, Carrie Belle, *The Life of Thomas J. Rusk*, Thesis for M. A. Degree, University of Texas Library; also copy in Stephen F. Austin State University Library.

Texas Almanac of 1858, from *A Compendium of Texas History*, compiled by Day, James M., Texian Press, Waco, 1967.

Tolbert, Frank X., in *Dallas Morning News*, Oct. 25, 1965.

Tolbert, Frank X., *The Day of San Jacinto*, McGraw-Hill Book Co., Inc., New York, 1959. Used with permission of Publisher.

Williams, Amelia W., and Barker, Eugene C., Eds., *The Writings of Sam Houston, 1813-1862*, University of Texas Press, Austin, 1938.

Wisehart, M. K., *Sam Houston, American Giant*, Robert B. Luce, Inc., Washington, D. C., 1962.

Wortham, Louis J., *A History of Texas*, Wortham-Molyneaux Co., Fort Worth, 1924.

Yoakum, Henderson K., *History of Texas*, Redfield Publishers, New York, 1855.

Index

188

189

44280

J. M. HODGES LEARNING CENTER
WHARTON COUNTY JUNIOR COLLEGE
WHARTON, TEXAS 77488

Wharton, John A., Adjutant General, 40; 45, 67; duel with William T. Astin, 82
Wharton, William M., 15
Wheeler, Royal T., 122
"Whip-Handle Dispatch," 62
Wiley, Rusk slave, 162, 171
Wilson, Robert, 100

Woll affair, 60
Wyatt, Mildred, vii, 169n

Y

"Yellowstone" ship, 38, 55

Z

Zavala, Lorenzo de, 33, 34
Zavala, Lorenzo de, Jr., 51